DANISH YEARBOOK
OF
PHILOSOPHY

VOLUME 43

DANISH YEARBOOK OF PHILOSOPHY

VOLUME 43
2008

MUSEUM TUSCULANUM PRESS
UNIVERSITY OF COPENHAGEN 2009

Published for
Dansk Filosofisk Selskab
in cooperation with
the Philosophical Societies of Aarhus and Odense
and with financial support from
the Danish Research Council for the Humanities

*

EDITORIAL BOARD:

FINN COLLIN
University of Copenhagen
Chairman

JØRGEN HUGGLER
Danish University of Education

UFFE JUUL JENSEN
University of Aarhus

STIG ANDUR PEDERSEN
Roskilde University Centre

ERICH KLAWONN
Odense University

HANS SIGGAARD JENSEN
Copenhagen Business School

MOGENS PAHUUS
Aalborg University

LARS GUNDERSEN
University of Aarhus

*

Articles for consideration and all editorial communications should be sent in three copies to:
Danish Yearbook of Philosophy
University of Copenhagen, Department of Philosophy
Njalsgade 80, DK 2300 Copenhagen S, Denmark

Business communications, including subscriptions and orders for reprints, should
be addressed to the publishers:
MUSEUM TUSCULANUM PRESS
Njalsgade 126
DK 2300 Copenhagen S
Denmark

*

© 2009 DANISH YEARBOOK OF PHILOSOPHY
COPENHAGEN, DENMARK
PRINTED IN DENMARK
BY SPECIAL-TRYKKERIET VIBORG A-S

ISBN 978 87 635 2582 4
ISSN 0070 2749

CONTENTS

Kaj Børge Hansen: *Remarks on Wittgenstein's Philosophy: Philosophical Method and Contradictions* 7-40

Pelle G. Hansen: *Why Mixed Equilibria May Not Be Conventions* 41-68

Asger Sørensen: *Deontology – Born and Kept in Servitude by Utilitarianism*.. 69-96

Sune Frølund: *Body and Motion in Early Modern Philosophy of Nature: Newton against Descartes*... 97-118

REMARKS ON WITTGENSTEIN'S PHILOSOPHY: PHILOSOPHICAL METHOD AND CONTRADICTIONS

KAJ BØRGE HANSEN

Uppsala University

ABSTRACT. This essay is a critical analysis of some themes in Wittgenstein's later philosophy. It is not primarily Wittgenstein-exegesis. Much more modestly, my purpose is to express my own thoughts about some questions which Wittgenstein has treated in his writings. It is the second in a series of two articles. The first article, "Remarks on Wittgenstein's Philosophy: Private Language and Meaning", was published in Volume 42, 2007, of the present YEARBOOK.

Section 1, "Philosophical Method". Wittgenstein's conception of philosophy as language therapy is criticised. Instead philosophy is construed as foundational research. Wittgenstein's statement that mathematical logic cannot contribute to progress in philosophy is repudiated. Several examples of ideas and results in mathematical logic which have led to the solution of philosophical problems are given.

Section 2, "Contradictions: The Wittgenstein-Turing Debate". In lectures on the foundations of mathematics given in 1939, Wittgenstein claimed that contradictions in mathematical theories are harmless. A debate ensued on this question between him and Alan Turing. In support of Turing's standpoint, I use the theorem on Taylor series, Church's Theorem, and Gentzen's Cut-Elimination Theorem to show that Wittgenstein's standpoint is untenable.

For orientation, I also include here the abstract for the first article in the series, "Remarks on Wittgenstein's Philosophy: Private Language and Meaning".

Section 1, "The Private Language Argument". An independent argument is given for Wittgenstein's thesis that there is no private language. I show that psychological terms in ordinary language, in contrast to an implication of Wittgenstein's own private language argument, in their meanings do contain references to inner states, processes, and events.

Section 2, "Meaning". Wittgenstein's definition of meaning as use in the language is criticised. Meaning is instead identified with something in the content of a conscious mind. Applications are given to some suggestions in the philosophy of language by Chomsky, Harman and Fodor, Grice, and Kripke.

1. Philosophical Method

1.1 INTRODUCTION. During my early undergraduate studies in philosophy, I was forced to learn something about Wittgenstein's philosophy, both from textbooks and by studying excerpts from the *Tractatus* and *Philosophische Untersuchungen*. I was quite dissatisfied with the ideas and opinions he expressed; but nothing irritated me more than his ideas on the therapeutic nature of philosophy, that philosophy really is language therapy.
(* In the present section, the quotations are my own translations into English from Wittgenstein's *Philosophische Untersuchungen*.*)

1.2 QUOTATION. "A philosophical problem has the form: 'I cannot find the way out.'" (§123)

"Philosophy must not in any way change the existing linguistic usage; it can after all only describe it. It cannot provide any foundations for it either. It leaves everything as it is." (§124)

"It is not the task of philosophy to dissolve a contradiction by a mathematical, a logical-mathematical discovery. The task is to make the state of mathematics – the state about which we feel troubled, the state *before* the dissolution of the contradiction – surveyable. (And this does not mean that we shun a problem.)

The fundamental fact here is that we lay down rules, a technique, for a game and that then, when we follow the rules, things do not turn out as expected. That we are like caught in our own rules.

Our being caught in our own rules, that is what we want to understand, survey as it were." (§125)

"Philosophy simply places everything before us, and it explains or derives nothing. – When everything is transparent, there is nothing to explain either. Because what happens to be hidden does not interest us.

We might also call that 'philosophy' which is possible *before* all new discoveries and inventions." (§126)

"We do not want, in an unparalleled way, to refine or complete the system of rules for the use of our words. Because the clarity we are aiming at is in any case a *complete* clarity. But it only means that the philosophical problems should disappear *completely*.

The real discovery is the one which makes me capable of stopping the philosophising when I want to – the discovery which brings philosophy to rest so that it no longer is driven by questions which call *itself* into question. – Instead a method is displayed by examples, and the sequence of examples can be cut short. – Problems are solved (difficulties are eliminated), not *a* problem.

There is not *a* method of philosophy but rather methods – like various therapies." (§133)

"The philosopher treats a problem – as were it a disease." (§255)

"What is your aim in philosophy? – To show the fly the way out of the flybottle." (§309)

1.3 REMARK. (I) Thus, in Wittgenstein's opinion, there are two kinds of philosophy. *Traditional philosophy* consists of ideas and theories based on misunderstandings of the proper way language works. The real philosophy is *therapeutic philosophy*. It consists in revealing and clarifying in what way the proper use of ordinary language has been violated in a theory or idea of traditional philosophy and in showing that if the pertinent words of ordinary language appearing in the theory are used correctly, then the traditional philosophical problem, to which the idea or theory was supposed to be a solution, disappears.

(II) The following piece of motivation for the idea of therapeutic philosophy does not, as far as I know, occur in Wittgenstein's own writings. It nevertheless appears to me to be the reasoning which, wittingly or unwittingly, is behind Wittgenstein's view. There are some premises:

(3-1) *All philosophical problems are purely conceptual problems.*
(3-2) *Concepts are meanings.*
(3-3) *Meaning is use in the language.*

Premise (3-1) is a basic assumption in analytic philosophy. Wittgenstein has probably taken it over from Moore and Russell. Concerning (3-2), it is a common opinion among analytic philosophers that meanings and concepts are the same. Premise (3-3) is Wittgenstein's own theory of meaning. In Section 2 of

"Remarks on Wittgenstein's Philosophy: Private Language and Meaning", I showed that it is a consequence of the private language argument which is thus the support of the whole of Wittgenstein's later philosophy. When this argument does not hold, the whole edifice collapses.

Consider a philosophical problem Π. According to the first premise, Π is a purely conceptual problem. To solve it, we need only consider concepts. By the premises (3-2) and (3-3) together, concepts can be identified with use in the language. Therefore Π is a problem about the use in the language of the expressions in the formulation of Π. The terms occurring in the formulation of Π are of two sorts: terms from ordinary language and technical terms. But to be intelligible, all technical terms must ultimately be definable in terms of ordinary language. Therefore the formulation of Π can be assumed to be in ordinary language. To clarify the conceptual issues in Π, it is necessary and sufficient to clarify the proper use in ordinary language of the expressions occurring in the formulation of Π because this use exactly represents the meaning and hence the concept. The latter idea was effectively formulated by Wittgenstein's student Norman Malcolm in a slogan.

Proposition *(Wittgenstein-Malcolm)*. Ordinary language makes no mistakes.

PROOF:
The impact of the statement is that no matter how an expression is used in ordinary language, this use cannot attach an incorrect meaning, and therefore not an incorrect concept either, to the expression. The reason for this is that the meaning *is* the use, the whole use, and nothing but the use in ordinary language.

Studying language use, we have now completely elucidated the concepts occurring in the formulation of the problem Π. Wittgenstein's contention is that with this clarification, the problem Π dissolves and disappears. It was a pseudo-problem and its dissolution results in no philosophical theory. To draw this conclusion, he apparently needs one more assumption:

(3-4)   *A body of knowledge about language-use is not a philosophical theory.*

1.4 REMARK. (I) In my opinion, a philosopher should ask the fundamental questions about our existence. A philosopher should ask questions about reality, not only about language and language use. To philosophise is to strive for some understanding of this puzzling existence. This makes philosophy a great and worthwhile endeavour. Wittgenstein's view on philosophy, that its problems only are the result of linguistic misunderstandings, makes a trifling matter of it. To spend a life making philosophical problems evaporate by disentangling such misunderstandings is a sure way to waste one's life.

(II) In the essay "What is Philosophy?" in my book *Applied Logic* (1996), I investigate the nature of philosophy. The answer given is that philosophical problems are foundational problems; philosophy is foundational studies. The foundations can be of many different kinds: foundations of mathematics, of physics, of science in general; foundations of politics and of social organisation; foundations of morals, of religion, of creative arts, and even foundations of life – to mention but a few. It is convenient to begin by studying the foundations of formalised theories of the sort considered in mathematical logic. The insights won by this study can then be generalised to other types of foundational studies.

Suppose we have a non-empirical problem Π. Sometimes such a problem can be solved in an established axiomatisable theory T. The solution consists in deriving in T a solution B to the problem. Sometimes the problem Π cannot be solved in any existing theory. To solve the problem, we have to find one or more new, true assumptions $A_1, A_2, \ldots$ to add as axioms to an existing axiomatised and true theory T such that $T \cup \{A_1, A_2, \ldots\}$ implies a solution to Π. If Π is solvable in T, we have a recursive proof predicate by which the correctness of the solution can be checked. In the case where we need new assumptions $A_1, A_2, \ldots$, there is no recursive proof predicate by which $A_1, A_2, \ldots$ can be verified. We must use other methods, for instance conceptual analysis or speculation and insights. These are methods traditionally associated with philosophy. Since there are only two kinds of problems – those which can be solved in an existing theory and those which cannot – we can identify philosophical problems with the latter sort. But the basic principles of a theory are its foundations. Therefore philosophical problems are foundational problems. I give some examples of philosophical problems which are foundational problems and cannot be made to evaporate by analysis of the proper use of words.

(1) A theory T which at first appears to be true turns out to be inconsistent. Find a way to revise the basic assumptions of the theory! An example is naive set theory. Cantor, Burali-Forti, and Russell derived antinomies in this theory. The solution by Zermelo was not found by analysing language, meaning, or concepts. It was found by studying the set formation process and gaining in-

sight into the structure generated by this process, the cumulative type structure. This insight then became normative for our concepts of sets and set membership and the use of the associated terms. The procedure was not the opposite, that the use in ordinary language of set terms determined the cumulative type structure, because ordinary language contains no clear rules for talking about infinite sets. Zermelo's solution is ontological rather than conceptual.

(2) A theory T can be incomplete in the sense that there is a problem Π which can be formulated in the language of T but to which no solution can be derived in T. Thus the continuum problem cannot be solved in ZFC (Zermelo-Fraenkel set theory with the axiom of choice). This shows that the continuum problem is a philosophical problem. For the same reason as in the preceding example, analysis of ordinary language cannot help here.

(3) Something about a theory is sometimes not well understood. Thus people have for centuries been puzzled by the amazing effectiveness of mathematics in physics. This is not a purely conceptual problem. It is an ontological problem which demands new insights into the nature of physical reality as well as a better understanding of mathematics.

(4) A theory sometimes does not satisfy a philosophical principle which is considered desirable. How to revise the theory? Thus Einstein's Special Theory of Relativity, in one interpretation, contains a convention, the so-called Einstein convention, which has observable consequences in the theory. A properly introduced convention should have no observable consequences. How to get an alternative theory of relativity without this undesirable feature?

(5) A theory may work very well in all applications. Nevertheless the theory is not understood. This is the case with quantum mechanics. Its predictions are verified with great precision; but it contains a host of predictions which are considered highly puzzling: indeterminacy, entanglement, apparent nonlocality, and the measurement problem, to mention but a few. How to develop the foundations of quantum mechanics to a point where these phenomena become intelligible and natural? Again this is an ontological problem and not a problem about the proper use of language.

(6) If ordinary language makes no mistakes and all questions of philosophy really are questions about language use, it is not possible to question the ordinary use of language. But this is often done in philosophy, for instance in applied ethics. In present-day established usage, abortion is not murder; but some people question this usage and see no reason to draw a dividing line between

abortion and murder. Present-day established sexual morals accept sequential monogamy, that individuals have many lovers but only one at a time. Consequently, the term "infidelity" is not applied to sequential monogamy in present-day established usage. But it is possible to argue that this usage is based on arbitrary and conventional dividing lines which do not exist in reality. It reduces morals to rule following – like in tennis: when the ball is on one side of the line, it is *in*, and when it is on the other side, it is *out*. In other words, the established sexual morals and associated linguistic usage have no ontological foundations. This shows that ethical problems can be ontological rather than conceptual and linguistic.

(7) In Section 1 of my article "Remarks on Wittgenstein's Philosophy: Private Language and Meaning", I examined the private language argument. Wittgenstein was seemingly convinced that by examining the grammar of expressions in a language apparently concerned with states, processes, and events in the mind, he had showed that such expressions do not contain reference to (naming of) such states, processes, and events. We found that Wittgenstein's argument for his thesis is insufficient. We also found, by using facts about reality – for instance the role of the central nervous system in psychological states and processes and the existence of self-awareness – that psychological terms in their meanings do contain references to inner states, processes, and events in the mind.

We see that ontological questions are not conceptual problems and, in particular, are not questions about the correct use of words in ordinary language. Generally, ontology, epistemology, and ethics contain problems which cannot be solved by linguistic methods alone. The same is true of some of the problems in the foundations of the sciences and in philosophy of nature. *Ontological philosophy*, the conception of philosophical problems as being basically ontological, makes philosophy a worthwhile enterprise. By asking ontological questions, we ask the fundamental questions about reality and existence. Ontological philosophy avoids a frustrating feature about traditional philosophy, for instance analytic philosophy: the endless discussions which lead to no or almost no progress. The task of ontological philosophy is to build foundations. Foundations can be evaluated solely from the superstructure which can be erected on them. A working superstructure validates the foundations. New foundations of mathematics should lead to new (and possibly better) mathematics; new foundations of music should lead to new music, etc.

1.5 ANALYSIS. If Wittgenstein's idea about philosophy as language therapy is wrong, then one or more of the premises (3-1) through (3-4) must be false. In the present context, I will accept the premise (3-2) to the effect that concepts are meanings. I look at the other premises.

Premise (3-4): This premise is false. Counter-instances can be found in Wittgenstein's own later work. He claimed that he did not put forward any philosophical theories or theses but only left reminders (about language use). This is not true. He did not himself live according to his own teaching. Thus, for instance, the private language argument leads to his claiming and defending two philosophical theses, labelled (4-1) and (10-1) in the exposition in Section 1 of "Remarks on Wittgenstein's Philosophy: Private Language and Meaning". He proposed a theory of meaning. He claimed that language therapy is the right way to do philosophy. (This is metaphilosophy; but metaphilosophy is also philosophy.) They are also philosophical theses. In contrast, philosophy as foundational research admits and demands theses and theories.

Premise (3-3): The assumption of meaning as use in the language leads to Malcolm's contention that use always represents a correct conceptualisation. We saw in Section 2 of "Remarks on Wittgenstein's Philosophy: Private Language and Meaning" that meaning cannot be identified with use. This opens for the possibility that we can question whether a given usage really represents the underlying concept adequately. This kind of calling in question is naturally considered to be philosophical. Example (6) in § 1.4 gives two cases in point from applied ethics. The general pattern is the following. Trying to understand the world, we try to identify sets of entities which are, by natural boundaries existing in the world, separated from other entities. Insights about such natural boundaries are philosophical (actually ontological) knowledge. Such insights may go beyond or question the correctness of previous insights. With the new insights, the perception of the world changes. Then also the prelinguistic concept and meaning change and the old use of the corresponding term is no longer considered adequate and is open to criticism.

Premise (3-1): This is the most difficult premise to discuss. The reason for this is the vagueness in the predicate "conceptual". Nevertheless I will claim that at least some ontological problems are not purely conceptual. According to Occam's Razor, one *should not* assume the existence of more types of ontological entities than are needed. A case of the use of Occam's Razor is Einstein's Special Theory of Relativity. In Fitzgerald's, Larmor's, and Lorentz's theories of electrodynamics, an ether is postulated. Einstein realised that this ontological entity could be eliminated and at least as good a theory of electrodynamics obtained by introducing instead the principle of the invariance of the speed of light and the idea of relative motion. But Occam's Razor, being a normative principle, is not purely conceptual. In my book from 1996, *Logical Physics: Quantum Reality Theory*, I investigate the ontological foundations of quantum mechanics. I find that in order to get a realistic and local quantum mechanics, the underlying ontology must be operationally defined. Here I use locality and realism as normative principles to select an operational ontology instead of, for instance, an ontology based on space and time. Again the demands of locality and realism being normative cannot be purely conceptual.

1.6 QUOTATION. "Philosophy must not in any way change the existing linguistic usage; it can after all only describe it. It cannot provide any foundations for it either. It leaves everything as it is.

It also leaves mathematics as it is, and no mathematical discovery can make it progress. A 'main problem in mathematical logic' is for us a mathematical problem like any other." (§124)

1.7 REMARK. A consequence of the last two sentences is that no discovery in mathematical logic can make philosophy progress. I now give some examples where results and ideas in mathematical logic have carried philosophy (in my sense) forward.

1.8 THEOREM *(Soundness and completeness)*. Let T denote a theory and B a sentence in the language of T.

(8-1)   T is consistent $\Leftrightarrow$ T has a model.
(8-2)   B is a theorem of T $\Leftrightarrow$ B is true in all models of T.
(8-3)   B is provable in pure logic $\Leftrightarrow$ B is true in all models.

1.9 REMARK. (I) Theorem 1.8-1 is useful in many contexts in philosophy. In philosophy of science, for instance, it gives a simple way of showing that a given theory is consistent: just find a model of the theory.

(II) Theorem 1.8-3 is extremely useful in investigations of the foundations of logic. It says that B is provable in the usual deductive systems for classical logic precisely in case B is logically true. This shows that the foundations of the deductive systems are sound and complete relative to the intended interpretation. It is nonsense to say that this is not an interesting and useful piece of information in the philosophy of logic. It has been questioned whether classical logic is sound in all applications, for instance in constructive mathematics and in quantum mechanics. A consequence of Theorem 1.8-3 is that this is only possible if constructive mathematics and quantum mechanics contain structures which cannot be adequately represented in the kind of set theoretical models used in classical logic. Again this is a useful piece of information in the philosophy of constructive logic and of quantum logic.

1.10 THEOREM. Let T be an axiomatisable theory containing Peano arithmetic.

(I) *(Gödel's first incompleteness theorem)*. There is a sentence G such that:

(10-1) If T is consistent, then $T \not\vdash G$.
(10-2) If T is ω-consistent, then $T \not\vdash \neg G$.

(* G expresses, interpreted in the metalanguage, "I, G, am not a theorem of T."*)

(II) *(Gödel's second incompleteness theorem)*. Let $Thm_T(x)$ express that x is the Gödel number of a theorem of T. Let $Consis_T$ be $\neg Thm_T(*0=1*)$. Then:

(10-3) If T is consistent, then $T \not\vdash Consis_T$.

(* $Consis_T$ expresses, interpreted in the metalanguage, that T is consistent.*)

1.11 REMARK. (I) Gödel's theorems were replies to Hilbert's programme. Hilbert's purpose was to develop secure foundations for classical mathematics. Let T be an axiomatisable theory of classical mathematics which contains PA (Peano arithmetic). Hilbert divides T in a *finitistic* part and an *abstract* part. The abstract part contains the sentences and proofs of T which can only be defined by explicit or implicit reference to the actual infinite. The finitistic part contains the sentences and proofs of T which can be defined without reference to the actual infinite. (This is Hilbert's *semantic criterion* of finitism.) The finitistic part only needs the potential infinite as scope for its quantifiers, as domains and co-domains for its functions, and for induction proofs. The finitistic part of mathematics is the important part, the *real mathematics*, since it can be argued that applied mathematics is finitistic. The abstract part of classical mathematics is not strictly needed, Hilbert believed; but it eases the development of finitistic mathematics and makes the development more smooth running. A finitistic sentence was claimed by Hilbert to have the form $\forall x_1 \ldots \forall x_n\ C(x_1, \ldots, x_n)$, which we abbreviate as $\forall \mathbf{x}\ C(\mathbf{x})$, where $n \geq 0$ and $C(\mathbf{x})$ represents a decidable relation. (This is Hilbert's *formal criterion* of a finitistic sentence and believed by him to be equivalent with the semantic criterion.) Universal quantifiers must be allowed because a formula $f(x) = G(x)$ in a mathematical handbook must be valid at least for all finitistic values of x, $\forall x\ (f(x) = G(x))$, for instance for all rational numbers. (Hilbert believed, erroneously as it turned out, that all such sentences $\forall \mathbf{x}\ C(\mathbf{x})$ are finitistically provable.) On the other hand, $\exists \mathbf{x}\ C(\mathbf{x})$ is not finitistic in itself. If $\exists \mathbf{x}\ C(\mathbf{x})$ can only be proved by an indirect proof, then there is no guarantee that the object which satisfies $C(\mathbf{x})$ is finitistic. But if there is a direct, finitistic proof of $\exists \mathbf{x}\ C(\mathbf{x})$, then it is inferred from $T \vdash C(\mathbf{e})$ for some finitistic $\mathbf{e}$. In that case, $C(\mathbf{e})$ can be considered the finitistic form of $\exists \mathbf{x}\ C(\mathbf{x})$, and $C(\mathbf{e})$ *is* of the form $\forall \mathbf{x}\ C(\mathbf{x})$ with n=0.

What Hilbert believed and wanted to prove was:

(11-1) If B is a finitistic theorem of T, then B is true.
(11-2) The finitistic part of T is self-contained: Every finitistic theorem of T (in the formal sense) has a finitistic proof in T.

Hilbert proposed that logicians and mathematicians should first try to prove *by finitistic methods* the following for pertinent theories T of classical mathematics – like Peano arithmetic, real analysis, complex analysis, and set theory:

(11-3) T is complete.
(11-4) T is consistent.

From the latter two theorems, (11-1) and (11-2) follow. Hilbert's reason to prefer (11-3) and (11-4) over (11-1) and (11-2) as problems to attack first was that (11-3) and (11-4) looked more tractable. It can be argued that all valid finitistic proof methods are present in Peano arithmetic and therefore are available in T. I now show that (11-1) and (11-2) follow from (11-3) and (11-4). To derive (11-1), suppose that B is a finitistic theorem of T which is not true. As explained above, B is of the form $\forall x\, C(x)$ where $C(x)$ represents a decidable relation. Thus the hypothesis is that

(11-5) $T \vdash \forall x\, C(x)$

and $\forall x\, C(x)$ is false. Then there is a finitistic **e** in the range of $\forall x$ which makes $C(x)$ false so that $\neg C(\mathbf{e})$ is true. Since C is decidable, $\neg C$ is. The calculation which shows $\neg C(\mathbf{e})$ is a finitistic procedure. Since T is complete and contains all finitistic proof methods,

(11-6) $T \vdash \neg C(\mathbf{e})$

But from (11-5), we get

$T \vdash C(\mathbf{e})$

which together with (11-6) implies that T is inconsistent, contrary to Assumption (11-4). Therefore $B = \forall x\, C(x)$ is true if $T \vdash B$ which proves (11-1). Define in T:

$P(x, y) \Leftrightarrow x$ represents in T a proof of a sentence represented by y
$\text{Thm}_T(y) \Leftrightarrow \exists x\, P(x, y) \Leftrightarrow y$ represents a theorem of T

Then we have just proved from (11-3) and (11-4) by a finitistic proof:

$\text{Thm}_T(*B*) \rightarrow B$ is true, if B is finitistic

Since T is consistent and complete and contains all finitistic proof methods,

(11-7) $T \vdash \text{Thm}_T(*B*) \rightarrow B$ (* provided B is a finitistic sentence *)

by a finitistic proof in T. To see this, suppose (11-7) is false. Then by completeness,

$T \vdash \text{Thm}_T(*B*),\ T \vdash \neg B$ for some finitistic B

By (11-1), Thm_T(*B*) is true, that is, T ⊢ B which is incompatible with the consistency of T. To see that (11-7) has a finitistic proof in T, we note that Thm_T(*B*) is decidable because T is consistent and complete. If Thm_T(*B*) is false, then the calculation gives a finitistic proof of T ⊢ ¬Thm_T(*B*) from which (11-7) follows by sentential logic. If Thm_T(*B*) is true, the calculation gives a finitistic way of proving B in T, T ⊢ B, from which (11-7) again follows by sentential logic.

To derive (11-2) from (11-3) and (11-4), let B be a finitistic sentence which is a theorem of T. Then there is a derivation of B in T. Any derivation in T, whether abstract or finitistic, is a finite object and therefore represented by a finitistic term d in T. Hence P(d, *B*) is true. Since P is decidable, there is a finitistic proof of P(d, *B*) in T:

T ⊢ P(d, *B*)

Then, by a direct proof,

T ⊢ ∃x P(x, *B*)

and hence by a finitistic proof

T ⊢ Thm_T(*B*)

Then, by (11-7), we have by a finitistic proof

T ⊢ B

which verifies (11-2).

This then is Hilbert's programme: Prove (11-3) and (11-4)! These results will verify (11-1) and (11-2) which in turn completely justify the use of abstract methods in classical mathematics. This follows since (11-1) and (11-2) show that such abstract methods can never result in any false theorems of real mathematics, and they show that though abstract methods may be convenient and time-saving, we can always do without them if required. Hilbert starts with a certain philosophical conception of mathematics. Given this conception, he formulates the problem of the foundations of mathematics as a problem of mathematical logic.

Gödel's incompleteness theorems show that Hilbert's programme cannot be realised. Let T be an axiomatised and consistent theory of classical mathematics containing Peano arithmetic. Gödel's first theorem shows that T is not complete so that (11-3) is false and unprovable. Moreover, G is, according to Hilbert's formal criterion, a finitistic sentence so that T is not even complete as far as true finitistic sentences are concerned. The second theorem shows that T cannot be proven consistent using only the methods available in T. Since T contains all finitistic proof methods, T cannot be proven consistent by finitistic methods alone. Even Consist is a finitistic sentence, as defined by Hilbert's formal criterion. A consequence of Gödel's theorems is that Hilbert's philosophical conception of mathematics is untenable and must be revised or given up all together. This is a philosophical consequence. The dominant opinion is that Gödel's theorems completely ruin not only Hilbert's programme but also Hilbert's conception of mathematics. I do not agree with this. In my opinion, there are some sound components in Hilbert's philosophical conception of mathematics which should not be forgotten. Therefore a revision of Hilbert's conception is more relevant. In a revision process, Gödel's incompleteness theorems and recursion theory will be invaluable tools.

(II) Gödel's first theorem shows that mathematical truth (arithmetical truth, the truth of mathematical analysis, set theoretical truth) cannot be completely axiomatised. This is an epistemological result. Similarly, Gödel's second theorem to the effect that T cannot prove its own consistency is an epistemological result. The sentence G in the first theorem is not a theorem of T as shown in (10-1). But this is precisely what G expresses. Therefore G is true and ¬G false. This shows that mathematical sentences can have truth-values, in contrast to a widespread philosophical opinion. G and Consist are self-referential. The self-reference is constructed by the Gödel numbering. Self-awareness and self-consciousness are cases of self-reference. Gödel numbering gives a path to a better understanding of self-awareness and self-consciousness which are important in philosophical anthropology (for instance as used in Section 1 of "Remarks on Wittgenstein's Philosophy: Private Language and Meaning"). Self-reference may also be useful in epistemology. In the essay "Logical Rationalism: A Program" in my book *Applied Logic* from 1996, I have suggested that *a priori truth* should be defined as truth in all self-referential models. This might give a way to prove the existence of *a priori* truth. Details can be found in the essay.

(III) In the first theorem, neither G nor ¬G is a theorem of T. Then the problem whether G is valid or not is a philosophical problem. A new insight beyond the information in the axioms of T is needed. The interpretation of G as "I, G, am not a theorem of T" together with the remarks in Point (II) above show that this insight can be reached by self-consciousness. Thus self-consciousness can be a source of non-analytic philosophical insight. The inexhaustibility theorem shows that the foundations can never be complete. Since philosophy is foundational studies, this implies that there is not and never can be any "end of philosophy". Moreover, since G is not a theorem of T, G is not an analytical consequence of the axioms of T. Nevertheless it is possible by philosophical insight to see that G is true. This shows that conceptual analysis is incomplete as a method of philosophy. There are solvable problems of philosophy which cannot be solved by analysis alone. Therefore analytical philosophy is inadequate as an ideology of philosophy. Other methods than philosophical analysis must be allowed in philosophical research.

(IV) Wittgenstein has, in *Remarks on the Foundations of Mathematics,* a discussion of Gödel's theorems. A main point is his calling in question whether it is meaningful to say that a sentence like G is true without a proof of G. (This criticism is concerned with the interpretation of Gödel's theorems and does not touch upon the mathematical correctness of the theorems.) The answer is that it *is* meaningful for the following two reasons.

(1) G is of the form $\forall x\, C(x)$ where $C(x)$ is a formula representing a recursive set. The algorithm for $C(x)$ can be used to prove $C(n)$ for each natural number n. Then $C(n)$ is true for any n and provable in PA for any n, $PA \vdash C(n)$, and therefore $\forall x\, C(x)$ is true because $\forall x$ is meant to range over all the natural numbers and only over the natural numbers. This insight can be generalised and expressed in the infinitary so-called ω-*rule* for an arithmetical theory T:

$$\text{From } T \vdash A(0),\ T \vdash A(1),\ T \vdash A(2),\ \ldots\ \text{infer } T \vdash \forall x\, A(x)$$

The ω-rule resembles the induction principle. The ω-rule is, however, much more powerful than the induction principle. Arguably, the main difference between them is that the induction principle is based on the potential infinity of the sequence of natural numbers while the ω-rule is based on the actual infinity of this sequence. It is easy to prove by induction on the length of formulas that ω-*arithmetic* = [PA + the ω-rule] is complete arithmetic. Then all arithmetical sentences have a truth-value, in contrast to a wide-spread philosophical opinion. This is still another example of a philosophical consequence of a logical result.

(2) There is also another way to show that G is true. The way used in Point (II) above to show G true was to point out that G, *interpreted in the metalanguage*, expresses about itself that it is not provable in T. Since this is precisely what is proven in Gödel's first theorem, G is true (if T is consistent). This is possible because the Gödel numbering makes the formal theory T a model of T and in that model G is true. Let **M** be the class of all set-theoretical models of T. Let **J** be the class of all set-theoretical models of T in which G is true, and let **K** be the class of all set-theoretical models of T in which ¬G is true. Then **M** = **J** ∪ **K**. Then all models in **K** can be deleted from **M** by adding G as an axiom to T, and all models in **J** can be deleted from **M** by adding ¬G as an axiom to T. But T itself is a real and concrete model of T and cannot be deleted in the same way as the fictive and abstract models in **M** = **J** ∪ **K**. Since G is true in T (considered as a model of T), G must be considered to be really true and ¬G really false.

1.12 THESES. (I) *(Church's thesis)*. Let $f: \underline{N}^n \to \underline{N}$. Then

f is computable ⇔ f is recursive

(II) *(Turing's thesis)*. Every algorithm, whether numerical or non-numerical, can be represented by a recursive function.

1.13 THEOREM. Let $f: \underline{N}^n \to \underline{N}$. Then
 f is recursive ⇔ f is Turing computable

(* f is *Turing computable* ⇔ f is computable by some Turing machine.*)

1.14 REMARK. (I) The question concerning what information about a function can be attained by computation is an epistemological problem. By Church's thesis, such problems can be solved mathematically in recursion theory. By Turing's thesis, the same is true of epistemological questions about arbitrary algorithms.

(II) Church's thesis is not a mathematical result. It can be considered a philosophical thesis. If we combine Church's thesis and Theorem 1.13, we get the following equivalent form of Church's thesis:

(14-1) f is computable ⇔ f is Turing computable

While it is hard to give arguments directly for the original form of Church's thesis, Turing has given quite persuasive analytic arguments for the form (14-1). Thus Theorem 1.13 has transformed Church's thesis to a form which is more susceptible to philosophical arguments.

(III) Turing machines are useful models of living organisms and subsystems of organisms. In particular, they are useful models of the human brain. Turing machines are also models of computers and therefore part of the foundations of computer science.

(IV) In the traditional theories of definitions, a *real definition* of an entity states the essential properties of the entity. In contrast, a nominal definition states the meaning of a word. According to modern epistemology and theory of definitions, there are no real definitions. However, Church's thesis can be adduced as an example of a real definition. Combined with the standard definition of recursive functions, it states the essential mathematical properties of computable functions.

1.15 THEOREM *(Church)*. Let $L = \{0, S, +, \cdot, <\}$.
(I) The set of theorems of Peano arithmetic PA in L is not recursive.
(II) The set of theorems of the predicate calculus for L is not recursive.

1.16 REMARK. (I) Church's theorem expresses that theoremhood in PA and in the predicate calculus for L cannot be decided by recursive methods. If we combine Church's theorem with the Church-Turing thesis, we get:

(16-1) Peano arithmetic is undecidable.
(16-2) The predicate calculus for L is undecidable.

These sentences express that theoremhood in PA and in the predicate calculus for L cannot be decided in general by *any* method. All these results are epistemological results. They are proved in mathematical logic, and they can only be proven by methods of mathematical logic.

(II) It can be argued that epistemological problems concerned with what is in principle knowable or unknowable can only be solved by recursion theory. Epistemology is a branch of applied recursion theory. The idea here is that a human being essentially is a complex Turing machine. All epistemic processes in a person are processes in a Turing machine. Then the theory of Turing machines and recursive functions is the right framework for the study of epistemic processes and their results, that is, epistemology. Some questions concerned with what types of problems are in fact tractable or untractable can be solved in complexity theory and in chaos theory.

1.17 THEOREM. Let ZF be Zermelo-Fraenkel set theory and ZFC be ZF with the axiom of choice. Let CH designate the continuum hypothesis.
  (I) *(Gödel).* If ZF is consistent, then CH is consistent with ZFC.
  (II) *(Cohen).* If ZF is consistent, then ¬CH is consistent with ZFC.

1.18 REMARK. Jointly, the two theorems imply that the continuum problem cannot be solved in the established set theory ZFC. This implies that the continuum problem is a philosophical problem rather than a mathematical problem. The problem is to attain such new insights into the nature of sets and the set universe (the cumulative type structure) which will allow a solution. One possible kind of solution consists in insights which together with ZFC imply the assignment of a definite truth-value to CH. Another possible solution might consist in showing that the situation in set theory is similar to the one in geometry which is said to allow both Euclidean and non-Euclidean geometries.

1.19 REMARK. Gödel's theorem and Church's theorem give particularly good illustrations of the interplay between philosophy and mathematical logic.
  (I) Hilbert wanted to justify the use of the abstract methods of classical mathematics. This is an epistemological problem. It is a problem outside every established theory and therefore outside the scope of every established recursive proof relation. To develop foundations for a recursive proof relation for the problem, he developed a philosophical picture of classical mathematics. This leads to the formulation of the justification problem as two problems in mathematical logic: (1) Prove by finitistic (that is, indubitable) methods that PA and other theories of classical mathematics are complete, and (2) prove by finitistic methods that PA and other theories of classical mathematics are consistent. By philosophical reflection, Hilbert had brought a philosophical problem within the range of a mathematical theory with a well-defined proof relation, namely mathematical logic. Eventually, Gödel proved that the two problems of mathematical logic formulated by Hilbert cannot be solved. This has philosophical consequences for Hilbert's thought: (1) Classical mathematics cannot be justified the way Hilbert had hoped. (2) Hilbert's philosophical picture of mathematics is not tenable and must be abandoned or modified.

(II) Church's theorem starts with two problems of mathematics and of epistemology: (1) Is Peano arithmetic PA decidable? (2) Is the pure predicate calculus for the language L(PA) of Peano arithmetic decidable? Again we have problems without well-defined foundations and therefore without a well-defined recursive proof relation on which a definite solution can be based. The philosophical part of the problem consists in establishing such foundations. This part is solved by a philosophical thesis, Church's thesis. Using this philosophical thesis, the original problems can be reformulated: (1*) Is the set of theorems of PA recursive? (2*) Is the set of theorems of the pure predicate calculus for the language L(PA) recursive? This move brings the problems within the range of mathematical logic and a well-defined recursive proof relation. Church's theorem solves problems (1*) and (2*) definitely. The original problems (1) and (2) are solved to the extent in which Church's thesis is true.

(III) Philosophical problems are problems outside all established and well-defined foundations and therefore outside all established and well-defined recursive proof relations. Only problems which are solvable on the basis of an established recursive proof relation (or, more generally, an established recursive verification relation) are scientific. This makes the idea of a *scientific philosophy* – eagerly advocated by Carnap, Quine, and many other philosophers – an illusion. The foundations of science cannot itself be a science. 'Scientific philosophy' is a contradiction in terms. A scientific problem presupposes an established recursive proof relation, or an established recursive verification relation, on the basis of which it can be solved. A philosophical problem presupposes the absence of every established recursive proof relation on which its solution can be based. The examples given above show that this does not imply that solutions to philosophical problems are doomed to be arbitrary. There is no scientific philosophy; but equally well, philosophy is a necessary condition for science because there is no science without foundations.

1.20 REMARK. The examples with applications of mathematical logic to philosophy given above are mostly concerned with applications to epistemology. It is more difficult to find applications of mathematical logic to ontology; but there are indications that recursion theory can be used to solve ontological problems in the foundations of mathematics and in the foundations of physics.

1.21 REMARK. The list with applications of concepts and results from mathematical logic to philosophy can be continued indefinitely. Though philosophical logic (for instance modal logic, epistemic logic, deontic logic, dynamic logic) is much less relevant to philosophy than mathematical logic, philosophical logic has nevertheless helped to clarify a few issues in philosophy. (Wittgenstein presumably uses "mathematical logic" in Russell's sense and not in Hilbert's. In that case, "mathematical logic" in his mouth means symbolic logic and includes philosophical logic.) Game theory is indispensable in the study of the foundations of economics, in decision theory, and in the philosophy of action. Several branches of mathematics are useful and necessary in problem solving in the philosophy of science, in philosophy of nature, and in the study of the foundations of physics.

1.22 QUOTATION. "Philosophy must not in any way change the existing linguistic usage; it can after all only describe it. It cannot provide any foundations for it either. It leaves everything as it is.

It also leaves mathematics as it is, and no mathematical discovery can make it progress. A 'main problem in mathematical logic' is for us a mathematical problem like any other." (§124)

1.23 REMARK. Philosophy does not leave everything as it is. Philosophy is foundational research. Revision or amendment of existing foundations has an effect on the logical consequences of the foundations – that is, on the superstructure – and changes them. New foundations give rise to new superstructures. In the case under consideration, the superstructure is mathematics.

1.24 CONCLUSION. Wittgenstein's assertion that all philosophical problems arise only because of misunderstanding of the correct use of language is ill-founded. Then his idea of the proper task of philosophy as language therapy is also wrong. Philosophy is foundational studies: the search for truth outside established theories where no established recursive proof relation or verification relation is available. This leaves a vast field of problems for philosophy, including the traditional ontological, epistemological, and ethical problems. Wittgenstein's claim that concepts and results in mathematics and mathematical logic cannot contribute to the development of philosophy is nonsense.

1.25 REMARK. In spite of the shortcomings of Wittgenstein's philosophy, he is still very popular and admired. How is that possible? I think that part of the explanation lies in his ideas about the task of philosophy and about philosophical method. Though no qualified work in philosophy is possible without a mastery of the logical and mathematical methods of philosophy, he promises something else. According to him, mathematics and logic are irrelevant for philosophical thinking. The only competence a philosopher needs is to be able to speak his mother tongue and be able by simple examples to openly expose the rules of language-use, he asserts. Wittgenstein is the lazy philosopher's prophet. A department of philosophy which bans mathematical logic from its own curriculum and research – and almost all philosophy departments in the world do – dooms its own researchers and students to muddle-headedness and intellectual mediocrity.

This point is amply illustrated by the development of twentieth century philosophy. Frege and Whitehead-Russell were pioneers in the development of early modern logic. On the basis of their results in logic, they also made important contributions to philosophy. Taking their work as model, the programme of analytical philosophy was formulated. It was supposed that the logic of Frege-Whitehead-Russell – actually a fragment of it – sufficed for philosophy. The later development of mathematical logic was believed to be largely irrelevant to philosophy. As a consequence, the work of the leading professional philosophers became mostly marginal: Moore, the later Russell, Wittgenstein, Carnap, Popper, Quine. And after them came new generations of still weaker philosophers: von Wright, Dummett, Davidson, Kripke, and you name them. The foundational studies of Frege and Whitehead-Russell had degenerated into analytical philosophy. Instead much of the most important progress in philosophy from ca. 1925 and on, of which a few examples were given above, were made by mathematicians and mathematical logicians: Hilbert, Brouwer, Bishop, Zermelo, Fraenkel, Gödel, P. Cohen, Church, Kleene, Turing, Gentzen, Herbrand, Skolem, Tarski, A. Robinson, P. Lindström, MacLane, Eilenberg, Lawvere, von Neumann, Chaitin, Friedman, Simpson, and many others. The explanation of this phenomenon is that the logicians and mathematicians, in contrast to the professional philosophers, knew the relevant methods and results in logic and were able to apply them to philosophical problems. The key to progress in philosophy is to stay close to the development in logic and to foundational issues. The key to stagnation and regress in philosophy is to shun logic and foundational issues.

1.26 REMARK. It is of some interest that Gödel's theorem can be used to throw light on Wittgenstein's theory of meaning and the idea of rule following. To understand arithmetic, one must understand the meaning of the symbols occurring in the language L(PA). We define a *finitary rule* as a programme. A programme can, in turn, be identified with a Turing machine or a recursive function. I suppose that Wittgenstein, when he claims that language use is governed by rules, by a rule means a finitary rule. The relevant symbols in L(PA) to consider are the non-logical symbols $0, S, +, \cdot, <$, the identity symbol =, the connectives $\neg, \wedge, \vee, \rightarrow, \leftrightarrow$, and the quantifiers $\forall x, \forall y, \exists x, \exists y$, etc. The non-logical symbols and =, all represent recursive functions and relations. Therefore their use and meaning are determined by finitary rules. The connectives are defined by finite truth-tables so that even their meanings are governed by finitary rules. We consider the quantifiers. In the general semantics for a predicate logical language, their meanings in a given model M are given by the truth conditions in M:

$$M \models \forall x\, B(x) \Leftrightarrow M \models B(a) \text{ for any } a \text{ in M's domain}$$
$$M \models \exists x\, B(x) \Leftrightarrow M \models B(a) \text{ for some } a \text{ in M's domain}$$

We note that these truth conditions have nothing to say about whether there is any finitary rule in the above sense which determines the meaning of the quantifiers. In the case of L(PA), we are interested in the meaning of the quantifiers in the standard model for PA. Since ω-arithmetic is complete and has the standard model of PA as a model, we can study the truth-conditions for the quantifiers in the standard model by studying ω-arithmetic. We only look at the universal quantifier. The treatment of the existential quantifier is similar. The truth condition is given by the ω-rule:

(26-1) From $\vdash B(0), \vdash B(1), \vdash B(2), \ldots$ infer $\vdash \forall x\, B(x)$

and the falsity condition by:

(26-2) From $\vdash \neg B(n)$ for some n infer $\vdash \neg \forall x\, B(x)$

The falsity condition (26-2) can be derived in the pure predicate calculus for L(PA) and therefore is a finitary rule. Now consider the Gödel sentence G = $\forall x\, C(x)$. It cannot be proven in PA; but all its instances are provable in PA:

⊢C(0), ⊢C(1), ⊢C(2), ... A condition for using the ω-rule (26-1) in PA, at the object-language level, is that the set of conditions {⊢ C(0), ⊢ C(1), ⊢ C(2), ...} can be represented by one sentence. A computer programmed to prove theorems in PA can prove any of C(0), C(1), C(2), ...; but there is no way for it to ascertain the provability of all of C(0), C(1), C(2), ..., because this would imply seeing in PA the set of conditions as an actual infinity. Therefore in PA, at the object-language level, the meaning of the universal quantifier in the sentence $\forall x\ C(x)$ presupposes the actual infinity. In the proof of Gödel's theorem, at the metalanguage level, all of ⊢ C(0), ⊢ C(1), ⊢ C(2), ... are shown in a uniform way so that the set of conditions here is a potential infinity. The ω-rule (26-1) in the form

From ⊢ C(0), ⊢ C(1), ⊢ C(2), ... infer ⊢ $\forall x\ C(x)$

can now be used. But this presupposes that we see the formal theory PA from the outside. The provability of all the sentences C(0), C(1), C(2), ... can only be ascertained from outside the theory PA. In this case, the meaning of the universal quantifier in $\forall x\ C(x)$ presupposes that we see PA from the outside. To see PA from the outside means to assume that PA is consistent which in turn is equivalent with the assumption that $\forall x\ C(x)$ is not provable in PA. (This equivalence is a corollary to the proof of Gödel's second incompleteness theorem.) The unprovability in PA of $\forall x\ C(x)$ is a necessary condition for our statement that the meaning of the universal quantifier in $\forall x\ C(x)$ is given by the ω-rule. Therefore the ω-rule gives the meaning in the metalanguage of the universal quantifier in $\forall x\ C(x)$ just in case PA can be seen from the outside.

We see that the meaning of the universal quantifier in the Gödel sentence $\forall x\ C(x)$ in PA is given by an infinitary rule and not by a finitary rule. If Wittgenstein's opinion was that all language use and hence all meaning is determined by finitary rules, then the example shows that he was wrong. We see that the universal quantifier in $\forall x\ C(x)$ in PA gets its meaning from an infinitary rule which involves an actual infinity. To conceive of an infinite set as an actual infinity, we must assume that the set can be seen from the outside as an object and not only from the inside as a universe. This is the same type of operation as the one occurring in self-consciousness. It can only be done by a self-conscious being and in the person's mind. The alternative way to assign meaning to the universal quantifier in $\forall x\ C(x)$ is to see PA from the outside. Even this operation is of the same type as self-consciousness. This kind of operation, actually a hypothesis, can only be done in the mind. Therefore the meaning of the universal quantifier is, in the case under consideration, in the speaker's mind and it presupposes consciousness as in my theory of meaning. Then meaning cannot in general be identified with use and the following of finitary rules. Wittgenstein, to upkeep his theory of meaning, cannot allow meaning to be determined by infinitary rules and must conclude that the universal and existential quantifiers in some arithmetical contexts have no meaning. Consequently, in Wittgenstein's philosophy, sentences like $Consis_{PA}$ and $Consis_{ZF}$ have no arithmetical meaning – a repugnant conclusion.

To sum up: There are expressions, the use of which in the language is not determined by any (finitary) rule. Examples are the universal quantifier and the existential quantifier in arithmetic. This is a weak point in Wittgenstein's idea about meaning as use, and use in the language as rule following. Instead, the meaning of these expressions presupposes consciousness and a hypothetical operation which can only be done in the mind.

Occasionally it seems that Wittgenstein instead expresses himself as a sceptic about the existence of a definite meaning for a linguistic expression, due to the inability of rules to convey a meaning. Again the quantifiers in arithmetic can be adduced as counterexamples. Each of them has a clear and definite meaning, mastered by anybody who knows the elements of arithmetic. This is so in spite of the fact that there are occurrences of universal quantifiers in arithmetic which do not have truth-conditions determined by any finitary rule. Finitary rules and rule following are not as central and indispensable in meaning attribution as Wittgenstein believed.

1.27 EXAMPLE. (I) Towards the end of Section 2 of "Remarks on Gödel's Philosophy: Private Language and Meaning", I showed that Kripke's argument against the possibility of learning meaning via examples is not valid. Kripke's argument is based on a difficulty about the learning of rules (recursive functions) defined by cases from a finite number of examples. The crucial point in my objection to Kripke's argument is that definitions by cases in natural languages do not work the way suggested by Kripke. Here I point to another way of showing that Wittgenstein's and Kripke's suspicion about the inadequacy of ostensive definitions for the determination of the meaning of an expression is justified. I use the universal quantifier as an example and get the result as a corollary to Gödel's theorem. This is how Kripke should have proceeded rather than basing his argument on the primitive idea of definition by cases.

(II) One approach to meaning is to say that to know the meaning of an expression is to master a method which determines whether a given use of the expression is correct or not. In the case of the universal quantifier in arithmetic, to know its full meaning is to have a way of proving $\forall x\, B(x)$ if $\forall x\, B(x)$ is true and a way of proving $\exists x\, \neg B(x)$ if $\forall x\, B(x)$ is false, for any formula $B(x)$ with only x free. Gödel's incompleteness theorem shows that no such method can be learned by examples in the case of the Gödel sentence $G = \forall x\, C(x)$. To see this, we consider a slight generalisation of the axiom scheme of induction. This generalisation is equivalent with the standard form. Let $B(x)$ be any formula of L(PA) having only x free. Then the *generalised induction axiom* for $B(x)$ and for any $n \in \underline{N}$ is

$$B(0) \wedge \ldots \wedge B(n) \wedge (\forall x \geq n)(B(x) \rightarrow B(S(x))) \rightarrow \forall x\, B(x)$$

This axiom expresses precisely the definition of meaning by examples. $B(0), \ldots, B(n)$ are the examples. The induction step $(\forall x \geq n)(B(x) \rightarrow B(S(x)))$ represents the etcetera-clause relevant when the rule is clear. Gödel's first incompleteness theorem implies that $\forall x\, C(x)$ cannot be proven in PA. Therefore it cannot be proven by induction, and hence no proof method for $\forall x\, C(x)$ can be learned by examples.

All instances $C(0), C(1), \ldots$ of $\forall x\, C(x)$ are provable in PA. If Kc is the characteristic function of $C(x)$, this implies that all identities

(27-1) $Kc(0) = 1, Kc(1) = 1, Kc(2) = 1, \ldots$

are provable in PA. Thus Kc is the constant function which takes the value 1 for all natural numbers as arguments. The trouble with Kc in this context is *not*, as Kripke needs for his argument, that Kc is defined by cases, because Kc is not defined by cases. The trouble with Kc is that no proof method for all the identities in (27-1) can be defined by examples.

If the meaning of the universal quantifier in $\forall x\, C(x)$ cannot be learned by an ostensive definition, how *can* we learn the meaning of the quantifier? In Remark 1.26, I showed that one way of defining the meaning of $\forall x$ in $\forall x\, C(x)$ goes via a proof in the metalanguage of PA. Then we must operate in the metalanguage of PA and assume PA seen from the outside. Another way goes via a use of the ω-rule. Then we must assume the class $\{0, 1, 2, \ldots\}$ seen from the outside as a set. This ability to assume theories, sets, ourselves, and universes seen from the outside is not learned by examples and ostensive definitions. The ability arises in most of us when we are between one and two years old as a result of a genetic disposition and the interplay with other persons. Once the ability is acquired, it can be used to give meaning to new expressions, including 'self-consciousness', 'consistency', 'actual infinity', and the existential and universal quantifiers in arithmetic.

(III) It is possible to give a weaker criterion of meaning than the one used in (II) above. To know the meaning of an expression is to have a criterion which distinguishes between correct and incorrect uses of the expression. In this case, the criterion need not be a method which effectively distinguishes between right and wrong uses of the expression. In the case of the universal quantifier in arithmetic, this criterion could occur in the form of having a definition of $\forall x\, B(x)$ being true so that $\forall x\, B(x)$ is used correctly when stated if and only if $\forall x\, B(x)$ is true, for any formula $B(x)$ with only x free. By Tarski's theorem, the truth predicate cannot be defined in any consistent extension of PA. The truth predicate can only be defined in the metalanguage as, for instance, in the Tarski semantics. Thus, in this case, the meaning of the universal quantifier can be defined only if we consider the standard model of PA from the outside and relates it to the language of PA. The general meaning of the universal quantifier in arithmetic contains an implicit reference to self-awareness and cannot be defined ostensively by examples only.

1.28 SUMMARY. A widespread opinion is that Wittgenstein's later philosophy is only a collection of loosely related ideas and remarks. I do not agree with this opinion. The core of the later philosophy is a system with a firm structure and following a strict logic: (1) The foundations are laid by the private language argument. (2) The theory of meaning as use in the language is a corollary to the private language argument. (3) The therapeutic conception of philosophy follows from the theory of meaning together with a couple of other premises. This firm underlying structure is then coloured by superposing a wealth of remarks using an impressionist technique. This procedure bestows some of Wittgenstein's later works with much of the vivid spontaneity of an impressionist painting.

The private language argument, which is fundamental in Wittgenstein's philosophical edifice, also has a simple logical structure. (1) By definition, a private language cannot be used for interpersonal communication. (2) Since ordinary psychological language can be and is used successfully for interpersonal communication, it cannot be private. (3) If psychological terms had referred to something inner and private, they should belong to a private language. (4) Therefore psychological terms do not refer to something inner and private.

A weak point in the foundations of Wittgenstein's later philosophy is its fundamental building block, the private language argument. It is concerned with the philosophy of mind. The main purpose seems to be to disprove Cartesian psycho-physical dualism. For this limited purpose, the argument is essentially valid. But there is another philosophy of mind which allows the reference to inner and private states, processes, and events. It consists in identifying the mind with the direct awareness of the brain. Mind states are brain states, mind processes are brain processes, and mind events are brain events; they are these states, processes, and events as observed from inside the brain itself. The brain of a self-conscious being is a self-referential system:

(28-1) *A person P's mind = P's direct awareness (both act and content) of states, processes, and events in P's own brain.*

It is a psycho-physical monism. As shown in detail in sections 1 and 2 of "Remarks on Wittgenstein's Philosophy: Private Language and Meaning", the private language argument does not exclude this kind of philosophy of mind though Wittgenstein apparently believed so.

Equipped with this psycho-physical monism and with the private language argument disproved, one is not forced to identify meaning with use in the language, as shown in Section 2 of "Remarks on Wittgenstein's Philosophy: Private Language and Meaning". It can be shown that meaning should be identified with something on the speaker's mind. Ridded of Wittgenstein's theory of meaning, also his therapeutic conception of philosophy fails. Though the correction of conceptual and linguistic misunderstandings may be part of a philosopher's task, it is only a marginal part. Traditional philosophy is still meaningful and an essential part of philosophy. The central issues of philosophy are logic and foundational studies. Foundational studies include the traditional disciplines ontology, epistemology, and ethics. Mostly philosophical work results in theories, theses, and principles – and not only in the disappearance of misunderstandings as Wittgenstein claimed.

1.29 NOTE. The exposition of Hilbert's programme in Remark 1.11 is partly new and partly inspired by Kreisel's and Smorynski's expositions. Hilbert's ideas are faithfully presented; but the presentation is sometimes more stringent than Hilbert's own. The increased stringency is won by using notation and concepts from Gödel's article from 1931 on the incompleteness theorems.

2. Contradictions: The Wittgenstein-Turing Debate

2.1 INTRODUCTION. During the spring of 1939, Wittgenstein gave a series of lectures on the philosophy of mathematics at the University of Cambridge. Alan Turing was allowed to be present. Wittgenstein was concerned with the relationship of mathematics to ordinary everyday language. During one lecture, he considered the relationship between the strict notions of truth and falsity in logic versus the more pragmatic concepts of truth and falsity in ordinary language, including ordinary mathematical language. As an example, he took the presence of a contradiction in a mathematical theory. He claimed that a contradiction in a theory is not as serious as logicians used to say. Pragmatically we might go around the contradiction and isolate it, he claimed, and in this way avoid that it implies every sentence in the language of the theory so that the theory collapses. He was met with opposition from Turing and a discussion ensued between them.

2.2 QUOTATION. "WITTGENSTEIN: ... think of the case of the Liar. It is very queer in a way that this would have puzzled anyone – much more extraordinary than you might think. ... Because the thing works like this: if a man says 'I am lying' we say that it follows that he is not lying, from which it follows that he is lying and so on. Well, so what? You can go on like that until you are black in the face. Why not? It doesn't matter. ... it is just a useless language-game, and why should anybody be excited?
TURING: What puzzles one is that one usually uses a contradiction as a criterion for having done something wrong. But in this case one cannot find anything done wrong.
WITTGENSTEIN: Yes – and more: nothing has been done wrong. ... where will the harm come?
TURING: The real harm will not come in unless there is an application, in which a bridge may fall down or something of that sort.
WITTGENSTEIN: ... The question is: Why are people afraid of contradictions? It is easy to understand why they should be afraid of contradictions in orders, descriptions, etc., *outside* mathematics. The question is: Why should they be

afraid of contradictions inside mathematics? Turing says, 'Because something may go wrong with the application.' But nothing need go wrong. And if something does go wrong – if the bridge breaks down – then your mistake was of the kind of using a wrong natural law. ...

TURING: You cannot be confident about applying your calculus until you know that there is no hidden contradiction in it.

WITTGENSTEIN: There seems to me to be an enormous mistake here. ... Suppose I convince Rhees of the paradox of the Liar, and he says, 'I lie, therefore I do not lie, therefore I lie and I do not lie, therefore we have a contradiction, therefore 2×2 = 369.' Well, we should not call this 'multiplication', that is all. ...

TURING: Although you do not know that the bridge will not fall if there are no contradictions, yet it is almost certain that if there are contradictions it will go wrong somewhere.

WITTGENSTEIN: But nothing has ever gone wrong that way yet. ..."

(* From Andrew Hodges' *Alan Turing: The Enigma* (1983). The same piece of conversation is reconstructed in Cora Diamond (editor, 1976), *Wittgenstein's Lectures on the Foundations of Mathematics, 1939*. There are a few minor differences in the formulations; but in content, the two expositions agree.*)

2.3 REMARK. The general opinion, except possibly among Wittgensteinians, is that Wittgenstein fell wide of the mark here and that Turing won the debate. I now advance three observations which show that Turing was, indeed, right.

2.4 THEOREM *(Taylor's formula)*. (I) Let $f: \underline{R} \to \underline{R}$ be n times continuously differentiable in an open interval I around 0. Then for all $x \in I$:

(4-1) $f(x) = f(0) + [f'(0)/1!] x + [f''(0)/2!] x^2 + \ldots + [f^{(n-1)}(0)/(n-1)!] x^{n-1}$

$ + R_n(x)$

(II) If $f: \underline{R} \to \underline{R}$ is infinitely many times differentiable in I and if for all $x \in I$ $R_n(x) \to 0$ when $n \to \infty$, then

(4-2) $f(x) = f(0) + [f'(0)/1!] x + [f''(0)/2!] x^2 + \ldots + [f^{(n)}(0)/n!] x^n + \ldots$

2.5 REMARK. Wittgenstein apparently believes that all calculations in applied mathematics are of the type 2×2 = 4 and that something like 2×2 = 369 always comes as an immediate consequence of a contradiction in an inconsistent theory and therefore is easy to recognise. This is a misunderstanding. The usual pattern of doing calculations in, for instance, engineering is to find a suitable theorem in the mathematical theory and use it to simplify the calculation. A simple example is Taylor's formula. From (4-2), we get for instance:

(5-1) $\quad e^x = 1 + x + x^2/2! + x^3/3! + \ldots$
(5-2) $\quad \sin x = x - x^3/3! + x^5/5! - x^7/7! + \ldots$

Truncating and using only, e.g., the first four terms, e^x and $\sin x$ can be calculated with good approximation in a neighbourhood of 0. Now suppose that the mathematical theory is inconsistent. Then also the following formula can be derived in the theory (because anything can be derived):

(5-3) $\quad f(x) = f(0) + f'(0) x + f''(0) x^2 + \ldots + f^{(n)}(0) x^n + \ldots$

This results in the "Taylor series expansions" for e^x and $\sin x$:

(5-4) $\quad e^x = 1 + x + x^2 + x^3 + \ldots$
(5-5) $\quad \sin x = x - x^3 + x^5 - x^7 + \ldots$

If an engineer approximates e^x and $\sin x$ by using the formulas (5-4) and (5-5), he might easily get values which deviate sufficiently from the correct values to result in an unstable bridge, for instance when making a calculation of the strength of material – just as suggested by Turing.

2.6 REMARK. The inference pattern used to derive any sentence from a contradiction is

(6-1) $\quad \bot \vdash B$

where $\bot$ is an arbitrary contradiction, that is, an arbitrary logically false sentence. In the present context, Wittgenstein must be able to block *all* inferences of the form (6-1). For him to be able to do that, there must be an algorithm which can recognise all contradictions and distinguish them from satisfiable sentences. Wittgenstein apparently assumes that ⊥ always is of the form (A ∧ ¬A) which *can* be algorithmically recognised. But this is an erroneous assumption. ⊥ can be any logically false sentence.

We consider the language L = {0, S, +, ·, <} of arithmetic. Let **K** be the set of all logically false sentences in L, and let **T** be the set of all logically true sentences of L. I show that **K** is not decidable. First we define a computable bijection f: **K** → **T**. Let A be a formula of L. Then A = ¬ ...¬ B for some formula B whose leftmost symbol is not '¬'. We call the sequence of negation signs to the left of B for the *negation matrix* of A. The negation matrix may be empty. Let **O** be the set of formulas of L with an odd number of '¬' in the negation matrix, and let **E** be the set of formulas with an even number of '¬' in the negation matrix. If A has a non-empty negation matrix, then let A_R denote the result of removing one negation sign from the negation matrix. We can now define the mapping f:

$f(A) = ¬A$ if A∈**E**
$f(A) = A_R$ if A∈**O**

f is clearly a computable bijection of **K** and **T**. If **K** were decidable, then the decision procedure for **K** together with the computation method for f should give a decision method for **T**. By Church's thesis, **T** should be recursive which contradicts Church's theorem 1.15(II). Therefore **K** is not decidable and Wittgenstein will not in general be able to recognise whether a derivation of a sentence B has gone via a contradiction or not.

2.7 Sequent calculus. We consider an inconsistent theory T. If T is inconsistent, then a finite subset Γ = {A_1, ..., A_n} of the axioms of T is inconsistent. We can therefore assume that Γ = {A_1, ..., A_n} contains all the axioms of T. Let the deductive machinery of T be the sequent calculus SK. We assume that we have the standard formulation of the sequent calculus. The selection of rules from SK we need here are:

From Γ ⊢ Δ infer Γ ⊢ A, Δ (Weakening)
From Γ', A, B, Γ" ⊢ Δ infer Γ', B, A, Γ" ⊢ Δ (Exchange)
From Γ, A, A ⊢ Δ infer Γ, A ⊢ Δ (Contraction)
From Γ ⊢ A, Δ and Λ, A ⊢ Π infer Γ, Λ ⊢ Δ, Π (Cut)

A deduction is called *cut-free* if it contains no applications of the Cut-rule.

2.8 THEOREM *(Gentzen's Cut-Elimination theorem)*. If there is a deduction in SK of $\Gamma \vdash \Delta$, then there is a cut-free deduction of $\Gamma \vdash \Delta$ in SK.

2.9 REMARK. If T is inconsistent, then any sentence B is provable in T. Wittgenstein apparently believes that any such proof must go via a contradiction of the form $(A \wedge \neg A)$ and use the logically valid inference pattern

$$A, \neg A \vdash B$$

In the sequent calculus, this inference pattern can be proven valid by using the Cut-rule. By hypothesis, T is inconsistent. Therefore we can, for some sentence A, prove in SK:

(9-1) $\Gamma \vdash A$
(9-2) $\Gamma, A \vdash$

where (9-2) expresses that $\neg A$ is a consequence of Γ. From (9-1),

(9-3) $\Gamma \vdash A, B$ (* Weakening *)

Then from (9-2) and (9-3),

$\Gamma, \Gamma \vdash B$ (* Cut *)

Whence

$\Gamma \vdash B$ (* Exchange and Contraction *)

By Gentzen's cut-elimination theorem, there is a deduction of $\Gamma \vdash B$ in SK without any use of the Cut-rule. This is then a direct proof of B from the axioms of T without going via any contradiction of the form $(A \wedge \neg A)$. Therefore the inference pattern used is now

$$(A_1 \wedge \ldots \wedge A_n) \vdash B$$

It is easy to see that $(A_1 \wedge ... \wedge A_n)$ can be any contradiction in the language of T. As shown in Remark 2.6, there is no algorithm which in general can decide whether $(A_1 \wedge ... \wedge A_n)$ is a contradiction or not, and therefore there is no method for blocking the derivation of B from the axioms of T; but such a method is what Wittgenstein needs for his idea.

2.10 REMARK. It seems that Turing in the following quotation actually hints at Gentzen's cut-elimination theorem without being explicit. This is perfectly possible since Gentzen's theorem was published in 1934 and must have been known to Turing.

2.11 QUOTATION. The discussion between Turing and Wittgenstein, of which a fragment was quoted in §2.2, ends with the following altercation:
"WITTGENSTEIN: You might get p.~p by means of Frege's system. If you can draw any conclusion you like from it, then that, as far as I can see, is all the trouble you can get into. And I would say, 'Well then, just don't draw any conclusions from a contradiction.'
TURING: But that would not be enough. For if one made that rule, one could get around it and get any conclusion one liked without actually going through the contradiction.
WITTGENSTEIN: Well, we must continue this discussion next time."
(* From Cora Diamond (editor, 1976), *Wittgenstein's Lectures on the Foundations of Mathematics, 1939.**)

2.12 REMARK. Some of Wittgenstein's statements in the debate show a curious ignorance about the nature of mathematical work. He seems erroneously to have believed that all calculations in applied mathematics consist in using simple algorithms like a multiplication algorithm. However, the common way to make a calculation in, for instance, engineering is to get the result as a corollary to a theorem of mathematics. The example in §§ 2.4-2.5 shows calculations as corollaries to the theorem on the Taylor formula. Numerous other examples can be given. One wonders what he did during the years he studied engineering. Apparently, he also believed that foundational systems like Frege's and Cantor's are used in applied mathematics to solve computational problems. This is a misunderstanding. The theories actually used – like arithmetic, algebra, geometry, real and complex analysis, the theory of ordinary and partial differential equations, and functional analysis – are independent of the foundational systems. Moreover, these theories are consistent, and that is why "nothing has ever gone wrong that way yet."

2.13 CONCLUSION. Wittgenstein's idea that contradictions are harmless in ordinary mathematics is untenable. While Wittgenstein's ideas on private language and on meaning at least initially may have some plausibility, his thoughts about the harmlessness of contradictions in mathematical theories are primitive and amateurish.

2.14 EXAMPLE. It might be of some interest that there are examples of theories, namely ω-inconsistent theories, which to some extent are in the neighbourhood of satisfying Wittgenstein's intuitive idea.
An arithmetical theory T is ω-*inconsistent* if T contains an infinitary configuration of the form

$$T \vdash A(0), T \vdash A(1), T \vdash A(2), \ldots, \text{ and } T \vdash \exists x \neg A(x)$$

for some formula $A(x)$. ω-inconsistency is a logically weaker property than inconsistency. Referring to Gödel's Incompleteness Theorem 1.10, it is easy to show that $T = (PA + \neg G)$ is consistent and ω-inconsistent. It can also be proven that $T = (PA + \neg G)$ performs all computations correctly in spite of the ω-inconsistency.

2.15 NOTE. The use of Gentzen's Cut-Elimination Theorem in §§2.7-2.9 was suggested to me by Thorild Dahlquist.

WHY MIXED EQUILIBRIA MAY NOT BE CONVENTIONS[1]

Pelle G. Hansen

Section for Philosophy and Science Studies
Roskilde University, Denmark

ABSTRACT. In his Convention (1969) David Lewis defined conventions as behavioural regularities instantiating proper coordination equilibria made salient by precedent and operational by this being common knowledge. While later proponents of game theoretical approaches in the study of convention have agreed on dropping Lewis' eccentric 'coordination' requirement as well as that of common knowledge, they are confused as to whether conventions should be regarded as proper thereby precluding mixed equilibria. In this paper I argue that mixed equilibria may not be conventions, but also suggest that the reason for this reveals that though common knowledge is not necessary for a convention to operate, it may be utilized to identify the conventional aspect of a given practice.

Keywords: Lewis, convention, game theory, mixed equilibria, common knowledge

I. The problem

In *Convention: A Philosophical Study* (1969) David Lewis used the analytical tools of game theory to propose his famous theory of convention. This defined social conventions as behavioural regularities instantiating one out of multiple *proper coordination equilibria* made salient by precedent and operational by this being common knowledge. From the outset the theory spurred much interest, for several reasons. For one, it pioneered the application of game theory to social convention; a field at the foundations of social theory. Second, and perhaps more famously, *Convention* gave the first explicit analysis of *common knowledge*, the concept receiving its canonical formalization in Aumann (1976).[2]

Taking the former line of interest, an application of game theory to conventions like Lewis' is interesting as it promises a range of insights to social scientists and philosophers alike. The analysis of game theoretical models of conventions may teach economists what to expect or look for in situations of radical uncertainty; sociologists may come to learn how and why a seemingly opaque system of behaviour emerged and persists to exist; the political scientist how to reinforce or undermine it; and social philosophers may understand the intricate relationship obtaining between individual interests, spontaneous order and social goods. Most importantly, it may help everyone to clear the field of inconsistent ideas and hypotheses as well as reveal the nature and appearance of social conventions and their relation to other important phenomena within areas such as knowledge or morality.

One of the open problems in the field concerns the status of mixed equilibria as possible conventions. If unwinding the idiosyncrasies of Lewis' game theoretic terminology it turns out that mixed equilibria are ruled out by definition as bases of conventions because they fail to meet the requirement of being *proper*. ('Proper' is Lewis' own term for what is usually termed *strict* equilibria in referring to the idea that any player will lose from unilaterally deviating from a given strategy profile.[3])

Yet, ensuing analyses of conventions have revealed two general problems in Lewis' theory of convention ultimately putting this claim in doubt. First of all, it has turned out that the framework of classical game theory utilized in Lewis' analysis is insufficient for explaining the emergence as well as stability of conventions. Second, it has been shown that common knowledge is neither necessary nor sufficient in order for conventions to operate.[4]

The evolutionary and learning theoretical frameworks of analysis developed to substitute the classical framework in theories of convention have, however, succeeded in defending Lewis' basic idea that conventions may be analyzed as game theoretic equilibria, see e.g. Sugden (1986), Binmore (1993), Skyrms (1996), and Young (1998). But while univocally discarding the requirement that such equilibria need to be *coordinative* – i.e. that *no one* must benefit from anyone's unilateral deviation – they disagree as to whether the equilibria underpinning conventions are necessarily strict. Thus, while Sugden (1986 and 2004) has argued that conventions are necessarily proper equilibria, Ken Binmore has recently stated that they need not be by way of arguing that mixed equilibria, which by definition never are proper, may be regarded as conventions:

> The mixed equilibrium in the Driving Game isn't at all efficient, since the players who use it will end up in a stand-off half the time. But it is an equilibrium nevertheless, and hence available as a possible convention. I used to say that it is a convention that has never actually emerged anywhere in the world, until corrected by some Turks, who observed that I had obviously never visited Turkey. But I have now, and I see what they mean. (Binmore 2007, 62)

This question as to whether mixed equilibria are possible conventions is an interesting one. Whatever the answer may be, this will have implications for which structures may reasonably be attributed to a given behavioural system as well as for how to understand accompanying phenomena.

This paper will argue that ultimately conventions may *not* be regarded as mixed equilibria. Section 2 prepares the ground by restating the main tenets in Lewis' theory of convention relevant for the argument. Section 3 presents the evolutionary turn that has been brought to serve in the theory of convention in order to remedy the problems inherent in Lewis' theory due to the classical framework used by him. Section 4 discusses Lewis' definition of conventions as underpinned by proper coordination equilibria and rejects the idea of conventions as mixed equilibria. Finally, section 5 argues that the reasons why conventions may not be mixed equilibria reveal an intimate connection between conventions and the idea of common knowledge – the vague idea of which may have caused Lewis to insist on common knowledge as part of the definition of convention. In particular, it is argued that considerations of common knowledge may be used to identify the conventional aspect of a given practice.

II. David Lewis' Theory of Convention

Much in the spirit of twentieth-century philosophy, Lewis' *Convention* embarks on giving "an analysis of our common, established concept of convention" (Lewis 1969, 3).[5] But although self-consciously portrayed and perhaps even at times intended as an attempt at conceptual analysis of an element in everyday language use, it is obviously much closer to the construction of a genuine theory of the nature of a particular social phenomenon; or at the very most a conceptual analysis of a strictly *Humean* conception of social conventions. It is along the lines of this last intermediate interpretation of Lewis' aim that the discussion in this paper proceeds. To some extent this interpretation finds support when, in retaining the analysis as one of language use, Lewis himself admits that "perhaps not all of us do share any one clear general concept of convention… [but] what I call convention is an important phenomenon under any name" (ibid).

The idea of convention To illustrate Lewis' game theoretical approach to convention we consider first the most widespread and well-recognized example of a convention, namely that of the *rule of the road*. The *raison d'être* of this is usually and uncontroversially taken to be that of solving the recurrent coordination problem arising whenever two cars approach each other on the road. In this recurrent problem the drivers need to coordinate on which side to pass each other in order to avoid collision: *left* or *right*. Utilizing the tools of game theory their predicament may be formalized as the one-shot Driving game in figure 1.

Figure 1
Driving game:

		player 2	
		left	right
player 1	left	1,1	0,0
	right	0,0	1,1

In this game *player 1* chooses between the rows of the game, while *player 2* chooses between the columns. The first number in a given action profile identified by the intersection of each agent's choice shows the payoff to the former from this profile, while the second number shows the payoff to the latter. For now, these payoffs are taken to be von Neumann-Morgenstern utilities, where each player is assumed to maximize his expected payoff, without such payoffs being interpersonally comparable.

As is obvious from the Driving game it does not matter whether the drivers coordinate on the profiles *(left, left)* or *(right, right)*. Both will do equally well in solving the coordination problem at hand. Within the model of the driving game this is evident from the fact that both of these action profiles are *Nash equilibria* – i.e. neither player will benefit by unilaterally deviating from such a profile and hence it is considered to be 'stable' in the sense that no one has an interest in deviating.[6]

However, being *one-shot* the driving game represents only a 'time-slice' or *stage game* of the recurrent problem played within a population of drivers. Yet, coordinating on one occasion is different from coordinating repeatedly.[7] Thus, in this recurrent problem following some general rule of coordination will minimize risks as well as operational costs. For that reason we expect to find such rules whenever a coordination problem is recurrent and as a matter of fact such rules are usually and very easily observed in practice. Thus, in Denmark for instance, the rule is that we *always drive on the right*, whereas in the UK the rule is that we *always drive on the left*.

Rules like these are standard cases of what we tend to refer to as 'conventions'; a term distinguishing the phenomena referred to from mere *regularities* by incorporating a reference to the object as but one of several possible strategies for solving one and the same recurrent problem.[8] But where mere regularities may be explained immediately in terms of e.g. adaptation or optimization, the multiplicity of available solutions raises the question of what may explain conformity to one alternative rather than another over and over again. Here conventions distinguish themselves by calling for some kind of circularity or anticipation in their explanation: we conform because we expect others to conform as well. Relying on something like revealed preference theory, this suggests that a concordant stable system of mutual expectations similar to that captured by the action profiles of *(left, left)* and *(right, right)* underpins the behaviour in question; or more precisely, that general conformity to conventions such as *always keep to the right* and *always keep to the left*, respectively, instantiate Nash equilibrium behaviour.

Lewis on convention Utilizing a game theoretical approach like this in the analysis of convention, Lewis (1969, 76) came to define a convention as

> A regularity R in the behavior of members of a population P when they are agents in a recurrent situation S is a *convention* if and only if it is true that, and it is common knowledge in P that, in any instance of S among members of P,
>
> (1) everyone conforms to R;
> (2) everyone expects everyone else to conform to R;
> (3) everyone has approximately the same preferences regarding all possible combinations of actions;
> (4) everyone prefers that everyone conform to R, on condition that at least all but one conform to R;

(5) everyone would prefer that everyone conform to R', on condition that at least all but one conform to R',

where R' is some possible regularity in the behavior of members of P in S, such that no one in any instance of S among members of P could conform both to R' and to R.[9]

Given the nature of game theoretical analysis, the motivation behind this definition is quite straightforward. Condition (1) is stated for the obvious reason that for a convention to be in place, everyone must conform to R.[10] Condition (2) is stated as a reason of why everyone conforms to R, given condition (4) which states that R is a proper coordination equilibrium, plus the additional premises that everyone is rational, and that this together with (1), (2) and (4) is common knowledge.[11] Finally (5) delivers the necessary element that R is just one out of a multiplicity of available Nash equilibria of the game played thereby separating R from mere regularities; while (3) is another of Lewis' somewhat idiosyncratic requirements that everyone has to have approximately the same preferences regarding all profiles, which may be dispensed with.[12]

Lewis and mixed strategies Now, in elaborating on the relevant elements of the theory underlying this definition, we begin by considering the requirement that conventions need to be *proper* equilibria, as this is the requirement that rules out mixed equilibria as possible conventions.

As mentioned, Lewis' definition requires that a convention needs to be underpinned by one out of multiple proper coordination equilibria. Yet, if we return to the simple one-shot game of figure 1, there is a third Nash equilibrium. This is the mixed strategy equilibrium made available by allowing players to randomize over members of their strategy sets. Such equilibria are characterized by each player following some mixed strategy making his opponent indifferent between two or more of his strategies that are not dominated by any other available pure or mixed strategy (call this the "indifference theorem" for shorthand). Thus in the Driving game in figure 1 the mixed equilibrium is reached when each player randomizes with equal probability over *always left* and *always right*. In this case the mixed equilibrium yields an average payoff of 0.5 to each player and the strategy profile is an equilibrium since neither player can benefit from unilaterally deviating. Also, since nobody else benefits from such a deviation it is one of 'coordination'. But despite of this, the mixed equilibrium is ruled out by Lewis as a possible convention as it does not meet the requirement of being *proper* – while no player benefits from a unilateral deviation, neither does he lose. Now, keeping in mind that Binmore seems perfectly content with regarding mixed equilibria as possible bases of conventions, at this point it is already reasonable to inquire why Lewis precludes this.

In answering this question, the first thing one needs to notice is that at no point does Lewis explicitly discuss the issue of mixed Nash equilibria as possible conventions. In fact, at no point at all are "mixed strategies" or "mixed strategy equilibria" mentioned in *Convention*. How come? Reading *Convention* carefully one comes to suspect that Lewis did not consider mixed strategies as relevant for the issue in any sense. One observation that lends further credibility to this view is that although his notion of equilibrium is the standard one in the theory of games, he at no point refers to John Nash or the notion of 'Nash equilibria'. Remember, Nash became famous for proving that if games are extended to include mixed strategies, then every game has at least one Nash equilibrium (Nash 1950). Further, if tracking Lewis' use of game theory and his references it appears in many places that his primary source on the theory of games most likely was limited to Schelling's *The Strategy of Conflict* (1960). Though admittedly one of the best books ever written on game theory, this may explain the lack of a discussion of mixed equilibria as conventions. Remember, Schelling explicitly reserved the interest in mixed strategies to the issues of making behaviour unpredictable in constant-sum games on the one hand (ibid., 84), and in making incredible threats credible on the other (ibid., 175ff.). This suggestion on the limits of Lewis' approach is reinforced when noticing that while Lewis performs several calculations of the indifference points corresponding to mixed equilibria in *Convention* (Lewis 1998, 26), and uses these as separating points for measuring the difficulty of achieving coordination at one of the associated proper coordination equilibria, his discussion of *dominance* relations (ibid., 21) leaves out any mentioning of mixed strategies when it would have been both appropriate and more precise than the wording chosen by Lewis himself.

But if Lewis did not discuss mixed equilibria as possible conventions, then why did he introduce the requirement that conventions need to be proper equilibria? The reason is found in Lewis' discussion (ibid., 22-23) of some 'trivial games' with multiple coordination equilibria that he thinks should be precluded as conventions – see figures 2 and 3 below.

Figure 2
The trivial game:

		player 2	
		R	L
player 1	U	1,1	1,1
	D	0,0	0,0

Figure 3
Trivial game 2:

		Player 2		
		b_1	b_2	b_3
	a_1	1,1	1,1	0,.2
Player 1	a_2	1,1	1,1	.2,.5
	a_3	.5,0	0,0	0,0

According to Lewis these games are to be considered trivial since

> ...there is still no need for either agent to base his choice on his expectation about the other's choice. There is no need for them to try for the same equilibrium – no need for co-ordination – since if they try for different equilibria, some equilibrium will nevertheless be reached. These cases exhibit another kind of triviality, akin to the triviality of a case with a unique coordination equilibrium. (Lewis 1969, 21-22)

What Lewis wants in the first sentence is some kind of non-triviality where the players' choices are to be based on their expectations about each others' choices. This is not the case in figure 2. Here *player 1*'s strategy *U* strictly dominates *D*. Thus, the choice of *player 1* does not depend on his expectations about the choice of *player 2*, because *player 1* will play *U* no matter what he expects of *player 2*; and likewise, the choice of *player 2* will not depend on the choice of *player 1*, because she will receive the same payoff from any action no matter what he chooses to do. But in the subsequent sentence Lewis reveals that he wants something even stronger than this. This is revealed in figure 3, where under the non-controversial assumption of iterated deletion of dominated strategies as well as under the more controversial deletion of weakly dominated strategies, the choices of *player 1* and *2*, respectively, actually are based on expectations about each others' choices, yet do not qualify as non-trivial according to Lewis. Thus, what is at issue here for Lewis is not just that one's choice or expectations has to depend on that of the other, but that they in a some narrow sense have to be *determined* by each other in the sense of identifying one particular equilibrium – and that is achieved by requiring conventions to instantiate a *proper* equilibrium.

Salience and common knowledge Having established that Lewis requires conventions to instantiate one out of multiple proper equilibria and why (saving the requirement of 'coordination' for later), we turn to requirements of *salience by precedence* and *common knowledge*. Like the *multiplicity of equilibria* requirement, I will rely throughout this paper on the claim that both of these requirements – on the conceptual analysis interpretation – are intended to distinguish social conventions from other types of regularities.

The former requirement is intended by Lewis to capture the earlier mentioned and striking feature that conventions somehow presuppose past conformity in their characterization. Of all the alternative rules facing us in any new stage of the driving game, the one followed in the past will according to Lewis stand out from the rest by its uniqueness in this conspicuous respect.

Again, the inspiration comes from Schelling who coined the idea and rudimentary theory of salience with his discussion of and groundbreaking experiments on "focal points" (Schelling 1960, 53-80). Yet, Lewis' theoretical construction of salience differs in important respects from Schelling's idea of focal points. In Schelling's theory of focal points, salience is based on the search for some rule of selection that may suggest itself or seem obvious or natural to people who are looking for ways of solving a specific coordination problem. Different from this, Lewis constructs salience in two alternative ways: *primary salience* and *n-order salience* (see Metha et al. 1994a, b). Primary salience is the tendency to pick or notice something. *N*-order salience is the *n*-order expectation that others expect that others expect… that somebody picks or notices something.

Postponing to the next section the issue of whether any kind of salience actually may lead to coordination, it does raise the question of how such systems of expectations may ever come to be concordant or even formed; "what premises have we to justify us in concluding that others have certain expectations, that others have certain expectations, and so on?" (Lewis 1969, 52). It is here that Lewis formulates his idea of common knowledge.[13] Although the idea once again was one of Schelling's, Lewis was the first to give an explicit analysis of it and seek out possible implications.

According to Lewis a proposition p is common knowledge in the population G if a state of affairs A obtains such that:

1. Everyone in G has reason to believe that A holds;
2. A indicates to everyone in G that everyone in G has reason to believe that A holds;
3. A indicates to everyone in G that p;

where the relation of indication should not be taken as material implication, but rather as incorporating some kind of inductive inference (see Cubitt and Sugden 2003 and Sillari 2005). Clauses 1–3, along with suitable assumptions about the players' reasoning capabilities and inductive standards, then generate an infinite series of propositions such that everyone in G has reason to believe that p, everyone has reason to believe that everyone has reason to believe that p, and so on. For later purposes of discussion it is important to notice the role played by the state of affairs A in allowing the players in G to have common knowledge of p. This is said by Lewis to be the *basis* of common knowledge of p in G.

III. The Evolutionary turn in Game Theory

As earlier mentioned, Lewis' theory of convention stirred a lot of interest almost from the outset. To begin with, it was discussed within analytical philosophy on its merits as conceptual analysis. Soon its influence spread more widely to shape ideas within the philosophy of law, social philosophy and economics in particular.

However, after some initial difficulties in grappling with the relatively novel framework of game theory, some genuine problems at the foundation of the thesis began to emerge. While early interpretations had readily embraced the idea that salience of a precedented strategy profile followed from common knowledge of a successful precedent and of rationality (Grandy 1977), and that given such salience of a precedented profile coordination would follow (Heal 1979), it began to dawn that none of this followed on closer analysis.

On the one hand, a successful precedent in the sense of a series of successful combinations of strategies may be projected in infinitely many ways into the future. Hence any strategy profile in an ensuing stage game will be salient under some description of the precedented series of profiles (Gilbert 1989, 333-

34; see also Wittgenstein 1953). On the other hand, even if one particular strategy profile in a stage game could be determined as salient by precedent, then this would not give rational players sufficient reason to act in accordance with this, as the kind of instrumental rationality ascribed to players by the game theoretical framework is purely forward looking (Gilbert 1983). Although a rational player would surely want to play his part in the salient strategy profile if other players would play their part, he would also know that they would only play their part if he was to play his – but this is exactly what he himself is still trying to figure out.

Whereas the former problem can be dealt with, if only unsatisfactorily, by assuming an appropriate psychological nature of salience, the latter problem hits at the heart of the game theoretical framework. The multiplicity of Nash equilibria around which any theory of convention must revolve inevitably implies an equilibrium selection problem that cannot be dealt with in terms of rational anticipation. This problem is a general one for the theory of games, threatening the cornerstone of the framework. If, as argued by Schelling (1960), most games played in social reality comprise multiple equilibria, the application of the Nash equilibrium concept is undermined, as its explanatory as well as predictive power will be void in most situations. Even the most basic idea underlying the concept – that of stability – would be dissatisfying as it would eventually hang on the particular psychological propensities ascribed to the players in such situations.

However, during the 1990s evolutionary game theory spread like fire within the social sciences as a response to the equilibrium selection problem. This novel interpretation of the theory of games was originally developed within evolutionary biology during the 1970s and early 1980s in order to explain the evolution of animal phenotypes such as those involved in determining sex ratios or animal competition (Maynard-Smith 1982). Re-imported into the social sciences, though, it serves as an aggregate model of individual and social learning processes.

According to the Darwinian theory of evolution, a given phenotype persists only so long as it performs better in adding to the reproduction of offspring to its host than any other available alternative. If this is not the case, a phenotype that is better in performing this way is available on that point of the evolutionary path of the species. This will eventually appear and invade the population under the assumption that the latter will stay relatively constant in numbers, while the frequency of the higher performing phenotype will accelerate at the expense of the lower performing one. This dynamic is obviously one of optimization. But although the giraffe may have developed its long neck in order to reach the higher leaves, it is more likely that the evolutionary pressure for having long necks was played out in the competition with other giraffes, rather than by the trees getting higher. In other words, the reproductive success of a phenotype depends on its environment, and much of this consists of the group or population that its host competes for resources with. Ultimately, what follows from this is that, roughly, a configuration of phenotypes is stable only if its consequences are a *best response* to its environment, and as the environment consists of other such configurations, it is thereby suggested that evolutionary stable outcomes are related to the idea of Nash equilibrium.

The concept used to model this idea within evolutionary game theory is that of an *evolutionary stable strategy*. Following Maynard-Smith (1982)

Definition 2: An evolutionary stable strategy (ESS) in a symmetric two-player strategic game in which the expected payoff of each player is $u(a,a')$ when the player's mixed strategy is a, any alternative to a^* is called b and his opponent's mixed strategy is a', is a mixed strategy a^* such that,

- $u(a^*, a^*) > u(b, a^*)$, or
- $u(a^*, a^*) = u(b, a^*)$ and $u(a^*,b) > u(b, b)$

The first condition requires that (a^*, a^*) is a proper Nash equilibrium; the second that if an alternative is neutral with respect to the payoff against strategy a^*, then a^* does better against this alternative than it does against itself. This latter condition should be met in order to debar the phenomenon called *drift*: the phenomenon where the alternative b 'lies silent' in the population and perhaps ultimately overtakes the population by doing as well against a^* as a^* does against itself, but even better when meeting one of its own kind.

However, this is not the only example where the game theoretical approach as it developed within biology did not 'breed true'. Instead of approaching equilibrium behaviour as the result of introspective analysis by fully informed and hyper-rational agents, evolutionary game theory came to view equilibrium selection as the long-run result of a selection process in which mindless phenotypes play out their potential over time. In order to model such processes, evolutionary game theory approaches behaviour as the result of the same game played over and over again within a large population of agents on which some evolutionary selection process operates over time on the population distribution of phenotypes.[14] The most famous of these selection processes studied is the so-called *replicator dynamic*. This assumes that a population-fraction playing a particular strategy grows in proportion to how well that strategy is doing relative to the mean population payoff. However, such an approach does not only differ with respect to the interpretation of what a game is. It also presupposes that payoffs are interpreted in terms of something like interpersonally comparable evolutionary fitness rather than von Neumann-Morgenstern utilities.

Naturally, changes in assumptions like this one cause a lot of trouble if we want to follow the current trend of re-importing this enriched game theoretical framework into the social sciences. But such problems have been completely ignored due to the results achieved by using evolutionary models like the replicator dynamics for modelling learning processes on the aggregate level (see e.g. Sugden 2001). The need for such models stems from the fact that individual-level learning models such as fictitious play quickly tend to become too mathematically complex to handle (Fudenberg and Levine 1998). Especially if one wants to examine what happens when large populations of players interact, as is usually the case in the theory of convention. The temptation is thus too big for evolutionary game theorists, who work on the hope that ultimately the analogues between evolutionary dynamics and learning dynamics claimed may be defended successfully.[15]

The most important result following from this change of framework has been that it enables game theoretical approaches to account for equilibrium selection. When modelling populations of agents playing games with multiple equilibria in this way, the evolutionary dynamics are often observed to carry behaviour to particular Nash equilibria underpinning the conventions studied by Lewis. Just as important, the evolutionary approach to conventions does this without relying on some of the most problematic assumptions made in that theory. For one, it does not rely on the strong rationality assumptions that Lewis' theory is usually seen to share with classical game theory. Even with very limited amounts of rationality, if any at all, the agents assumed by evolutionary game theory succeed in coordinating on equilibria in the relevant games. Likewise, none of the strong knowledge claims that Lewis' theory shares with classical game theory and develops further in terms of common knowledge are claimed to be necessary for conventions to emerge. Without knowing anything else than the available strategy sets and sample results of past interaction, conventions emerge as a course of history.

IV. Conventions as Proper Coordination Equilibria

Now, getting back on track, remember that in Lewis' theory of convention condition (1) is fulfilled when everyone conforms to R. But everyone will do so only if this is rational given the expectation that everyone expects everyone else to conform to R (Condition (2)). This makes everything hang on condition (4): Lewis' claim that for this to be so R must be underpinned by a *proper coordination equilibrium*. But how does this claim appear when given an evolutionary interpretation, besides the obvious changes that must result from coining the relations between (1), (2) and (4) in terms of inductive expectations and the 'evolutionary' stability of these, rather than in terms of rationality and deductive expectations?

Coordination equilibria Remember Lewis' theory required not only of the coordination problems giving rise to conventions that they contain a *multiplicity of equilibria*, but that they contain a multiplicity of *coordination* equilibria; a coordination equilibrium being a strategy profile for which *no one* must be better off if anyone were to deviate. But this idea of Lewis' that conventions need to be underpinned by coordination equilibria is not only confusing – in the perspective of evolutionary game theory it also turns out to be quite unintelligible.

It is confusing because the concept of 'coordination' serves two different purposes within Lewis' theory. On the one hand it is used to describe the characteristic predicament giving rise to conventions, namely *coordination* problems. On the other hand it is used to describe a particular quality thought by Lewis to be necessary for any strategy profile underpinning a convention. This use is apt to confuse any reader at first.

More importantly, though, the evolutionary approach to conventions reveals that there are regularities that only separate themselves from standard conventions with respect to this feature, without it having any effect on their evolutionary stability. Thus, in one of the most important evolutionary interpretations of the theory of convention – Robert Sugden's *The Economics of Rights, Co-operation and Welfare* (1986, rev. ed. 2004) – Sugden explicitly dispenses with the requirement that conventions need to be coordinative, since it precludes rules such as those governing property rights to which Hume originally applied the idea of convention; obviously, if someone were not to insist on his property rights, then those who took advantage of this would be better off. But following Sugden in modelling such rules as pure-strategy equilibria in games like the Chicken game in figure 4, evolutionary analysis makes it clear that these are just as stable as any other convention. True, one party would become frustrated if it continuously turned out to be the disfavoured party to such a convention – wishing that others would deviate; yet, such conventions are still proper equilibria and hence stable strategy profiles the deviation away from which the evolutionary dynamics would assert a pressure against.

Figure 4
Chicken:

		player 2	
		Heads	Tails
player 1	H	2,2	0,4
	T	4,0	–1,–1

Still, one could claim that the notion of 'coordination equilibrium' does capture that interesting aspect of non-controversial coordination where nobody has an interest in strategic manoeuvres. But unfortunately, the associations of collaboration brought in by using the term 'coordination' for this aspect are highly misleading. Thus, for instance, since the notion of a coordination equilibrium only requires that *no one must be better off* (mutual weakness) and not that *at least one must be worse off from deviation* (mutual strictness), it follows that even equilibria such as the unique mixed equilibrium in the matching pennies game of figure 5 – a game of pure conflict – qualifies as one of coordination void of manipulative attempts.[16] From these considerations it is obvious why the requirement has been dropped in contemporary theories of convention.

Figure 5
Matching Pennies:

		player 2	
		Heads	Tails
player 1	H	–1,1	1,–1
	T	1,–1	–1,1

Common knowledge A further issue to be settled before dealing with the question of whether mixed equilibria may ever be conventions is the consequences that an evolutionary approach has with respect to the requirement that

(1)-(5) needs to be common knowledge in order for a convention to be operative.

Lewis' idea of the role played by common knowledge and the state of affairs *A* serving as a basis for this in the context of social conventions may once again be illustrated by the *rule of the road*. Imagine that *player 1* and *player 2* have coordinated 1,000 times by both choosing *always right* when approaching each other. This is the state of affairs *A*. Now, this will most likely give both players reason to believe that they have coordinated 1,000 times by both choosing *always right* due to salience by precedence.[17] That is, everyone in *G*, where *G* is *player 1* and *player 2*, has reason to believe that *A* holds. Also, according to Lewis, this state of affairs may very well indicate to both of them that they both have reason to believe that they have coordinated 1,000 times by both choosing *always right*. Hence, the second condition of definition 1 – that *A* may indicate to everyone in *G* that everyone in *G* has reason to believe that *A* holds – is satisfied. Finally, according to Lewis, that they have coordinated 1,000 times by both choosing *always right* may indicate to both of them that the other will choose right in the next stage of the game. That is, *A* may indicate to everyone in *G* that *p*, where *p* is the proposition that "the other will choose *always right* in the next stage of the game". Now, from this along with suitable assumptions about the players' reasoning capabilities, shared background knowledge and shared reasoning standards, the infinite series of epistemic propositions that "everyone will have reason to believe that the other will choose *always right* in the next stage of the game, everyone will have reason to believe that everyone will have reason to believe that the other will choose *always right* in the next stage of the game..." and so on may be inferred by the players using modus ponens and substitution, where the state of affairs that they have coordinated 1,000 times by both choosing *always right* is the *basis* for common knowledge of *p* in *G*.

Now, although this seems a persuasive account of common knowledge, as well as how it serves to make a convention operative given that the players go through these steps of reasoning, there are several reasons to be sceptical about it as a necessary ingredient of convention. Here I will only state one, but see Burge (1975) and Gilbert (1989) for others.

At home I have a heater in my son's bedroom. Every morning I turn it off before leaving for work. For a long time it would make loud noises in the middle of the night thereby waking my son and, hence, ultimately me. I didn't know what to do and tried all kinds of ideas and tricks. Always I would turn the handle and it would stop, but usually only for a very short time – except, as I eventually found out one night, when I turned it on '2'. I did not have any explanation why this was so and settled with a vague idea concerning the adequate amount of water-flow that my heater could circulate and hence always turned it to 2. Then, one day I met my downstairs neighbour. He told me that he had had the same problem with his heater just below, and that he ultimately had ended up with the same solution. Getting a plumber we learned that our heaters were installed in a way so that the only way they would work was by being positioned identically. Now, according to Lewis, my neighbour and I were not following a convention until we exchanged information on the staircase – well, in fact, until the plumber told us about the mechanics of our heaters. However, it became a convention the second he did (Lewis 1969, 75). Incredible!

While the point of this example challenges Lewis' theory of convention, it fits quite well with the evolutionary accounts. Here the individual learning processes of agents may lead to a gradual convergence on a convention solving their problem without them ever having reason to believe the state of affairs *A* leading to their success, reason to believe that others have reason to believe this, or that this indicates to them that others will conform to it in the future. Although it might not be the average case of a convention, this does serve to prove that Lewis' claim that common knowledge is necessary for a convention is in fact not valid.

Mixed equilibria as conventions Having come so far, it is now possible to treat the question of whether mixed equilibria may be regarded as conventions. As was pointed out above, Lewis' definition of conventions, as based upon proper coordination equilibria rules out mixed equilibria by definition. Though Lewis did not discuss mixed equilibria, what may be retrieved from his discussion of proper equilibria is that he believed this to be the case, as mixed equilibria do not fix expectations in an appropriate way. However, what may also be concluded from the above is that Lewis' reasons for requiring that conventions need to be *coordinative* as well as *common knowledge* are incorrect. The question is then whether Lewis' reason for requiring them to be *proper* is correct, in one way or the other given an evolutionary approach.

Returning to the driving game once again, where the mixed equilibrium corresponds to each player randomizing over *left* and *right* with equal weights, we may follow Lewis' line of thought and argue that in this equilibrium, expectations are not interdependent in the appropriate way. More precisely, as a mixed equilibrium is characterized by each player playing a mixed strategy that makes his or her opponent indifferent between two or more strategies it is essential to such a strategy profile that neither of the strategies combining in this are based upon expectations about the choices made by other players. To see this, imagine that *player 1* expected *player 2* to randomize in the way prescribed by the mixed equilibrium in the driving game, e.g. by her tossing a fair coin. Then *player 1* would be indifferent between his available strategies in choosing, as each would yield the same expected payoff. Hence, his play of this particular strategy would not come from an expectation about her playing this strategy. Likewise *Player 2* would be aware of this, why her choice of playing the mixed strategy would not depend on her expectations about the choice of *player 1*. Hence, if a convention was to be underpinned by the mixed equilibrium, it seems difficult to see how present conformity depends on past conformity as well as being able to induce future conformity.

However, from the discussion of common knowledge and convention, it followed that no kind of expectations as to each other's behaviour, or even existence, was necessary for a convention to emerge and persist. Hence, although we may be inclined to accept Lewis' reason for not regarding conventions as underpinned by mixed equilibria, this reason seems only to pertain to our ideas or use of language – to what we usually refer to as conventions, rather than to the phenomenon of convention itself. Thus, even if we deemed true that a convention should satisfy the requirement that in *principle* it must be able to be upheld by the kind of system of concordant mutual expectations required by Lewis' theory, we would like to know why and whether we are correct in thinking so.

Instead of following Lewis' line of reasoning, we may thus try to follow an evolutionary approach in search of an answer. Looking once again at the driving game, but now from this perspective, it immediately follows that the mixed equilibrium cannot be evolutionary stable. From the 'indifference theorem' it follows that a mixed equilibrium never satisfies the first condition in definition 2, but always satisfies the first conjunct in its second condition. Thus, a possible explanation hangs on the second conjunct of the second condition, and here it is seen that the mixed equilibrium of the driving game fails in this as well. Consequently, the mixed equilibrium of the driving game is evolutionary unstable, meaning that an alternative strategy may invade a population playing this game. To see why, imagine that a small fraction of players within a large population of drivers playing the mixed strategy begins to follow the rule *always keep right*. Members of this fraction will receive the same payoff as those conforming to the mixed equilibrium when interacting with these – i.e. 0.5 – but 1 when interacting with each other. Hence, the frequency of the strategy played by the fraction will increase as this will be copied by other players and using the replicator dynamics we find that the whole population will end up playing *always keep right* – one of the two evolutionary stable strategies in the game which turn out to correspond to the profiles thought by Lewis to underpin the possible conventions in this game, see e.g. Hansen (2007).[18]

Thus, at least for the Driving game, Binmore's claim seems unintelligible on an evolutionary approach. Still, if the issue was so straightforward in general, it seems difficult to understand why a famous evolutionary game theorist like Binmore could be that mistaken. But things are not this straightforward, as not all mixed equilibria are evolutionary unstable if we move away from the Driving game.[19]

Consider again the matching pennies game (figure 5). The mixed strategies combining in the mixed equilibrium of this game are evolutionary stable. Thus, any conjecture that mixed equilibria cannot underpin conventions because they are not evolutionary stable in general would be incorrect. But although the mixed equilibrium in matching pennies is stable, it is not a convention since there are no other evolutionary stable equilibria in this game. The question is thus whether there are more interesting cases of evolutionary stable mixed equilibria that may not resolve our question this easily? Now, consider the following *Telephone Tag* game (figure 6).

Figure 6
Telephone Tag:

		player 2	
		C	W
player 1	C	0,0	1,1
	W	1,1	0,0

The story of this game could be that the agents drawn to play player 1 and player 2 have their phone call cut off. Now, if both call back, C, the line will be busy and they will fail to coordinate. If both wait, W, the call is not re-established and coordination failure obtains again. Like in matching pennies, it turns out that the mixed equilibrium is evolutionary stable in this game. If a fraction should adopt e.g. the strategy C, then they will receive the same payoff as those playing the mixed strategy when interacting with these, but they will do worse when meeting members of their own fraction – namely 0. But one could also be inclined to think that both of the combinations (C,W) and (W,C) could be conventions, since they are by strict equilibria. Does this mean that we have found a convention that is underpinned by a mixed equilibrium? No, because as it turns out, the mixed equilibrium is the only evolutionary stable profile of the game as interpreted so far (Hansen 2007). But since Telephone Tag looks almost identical to the Driving Game, we are also inclined to ask why this is so?

The answer is found by noticing that while the Telephone Tag game is symmetric, its pure-strategy equilibria are asymmetric. This means that while the agents are not able to infer what position in the game they have randomly been assigned to – player 1 or player 2 – even if they know the way their payoffs combine, coordination unfortunately requires them to coordinate on different actions, rather than identical ones; and this is more difficult than the coordination problem in the Driving game since it requires fixed expectations as to whom does what. Working within the classical theory of games, Lewis tried to eliminate problems like this by claiming that in Telephone Tag one could just choose alternative descriptions of the actions available to the agents so that instead of describing the game in terms of the action sets:

$$S_i = \{C, W\}$$

we choose to the describe the sets as

$$S_i' = \{C \text{ iff } \textit{original caller, } W \text{ iff not } \textit{original caller}\}.$$

If warranted this would transform the game into the driving game.

In defending this transformation Lewis writes "But what makes the first pair of action-descriptions more natural than the second? And so what if it is?" (Lewis 1969, 12). He thereafter continues as if the problem were solved. However, it does not take much to see that the members of S_i are different from those of S_i' in at least one respect. The former are unconditional, the latter conditional. Further, the former description may be considered more 'natural' in the sense that it mirrors the *actions* available in the situation, while the latter conditionalize over these according to one out of multiple arbitrary features available in this. While every possible conditional must involve the naturals, the conditionals may have no other things in common and will be numerous. Thus, Lewis' transformation is both non-trivial as well as unwarranted (see Hansen 2007); and, if debarring the transformation for a moment, the mixed equilibrium turns out not only to be irreducible evolutionary stable, but also unique and therefore not a convention.

What if we allow the players to conditionalize? This, as Lewis claims, will transform the game along some arbitrary feature (ignoring here the problems arising from the multiplicity of these), making whatever symmetric equilibrium that appears evolutionary stable. Still, this does not make the mixed equilibrium a possible convention, because it follows from the evolutionary analysis that the mixed equilibrium is no longer stable.

It seems that the possibility left for defending a claim like Binmore's will be to argue that we may regard the mixed equilibrium as a possible convention since the mixed equilibrium may be stable in a population P the members of which are unable to conditionalize, while the pure strategy equilibria are stable in a population P' where agents are able to do so. Yet, again this move does not deliver the wanted conclusion, because now the populations are no longer identical. In P there is no other evolutionary stable equilibrium, while in P' the mixed equilibrium is no longer stable. Hence, although we may wrongly think so initially, there is in reality no alternative regularity to conform to in P, while in P' the regularity of conforming to the mixed equilibrium is not viable though we might be fooled by this initial thought to think so.

Finally, we could try to twist this argument by saying that an *expectation* within P that others do not conditionalize (and hence the mixed equilibrium be stable) relative to an *expectation* within P that they do conditionalize (and hence the mixed equilibrium is unstable, while the pure strategy equilibria are stable) would be a matter of convention. But once again the result is negative. The former expectation turns out to be evolutionary unstable as soon as the latter type of expectation is made available (see Verbeek 2002 and Hansen 2007).

Having come to what I believe is the end of this path given our account of the evolutionary approach so far, one could make a change of strategy and try a defence based on an alternative interpretation of mixed equilibria available within the evolutionary framework. Nothing in this framework implies that mixed equilibria necessarily should appear as the result of anyone mixing over two or more of their available actions. Instead a mixed equilibrium may come about in a game like *Telephone tag* by half the agents always playing *C*, while the other half always plays *W*. One could then say it would be a matter of convention who were playing *C* and who were playing *W*. In this situation anyone deviating would lose from doing so on average and thus would want to switch back to his or her original strategy. Perhaps this is the most viable account of mixed equilibria as conventions. Yet, such conventions seem rather to pertain to *how* a given mixed equilibrium is played, rather than to the equilibrium itself. That is, it is not the equilibrium in itself which is conventional, but the arbitrary partition of the members of *P*; or said another way, while it is a matter of convention that agent i plays *C* and agent j plays *W*, it is not a convention that the one plays *C* while the other plays *W*.

My final attempt to find support for Binmore's claim is by considering the tautological claim that if there is a multiplicity of evolutionary stable equilibria within a game, where one of these is mixed, then it would also be a convention. A straightforward attempt of giving an example of such a game would be the *The office game* (figure 7). Now, imagine that the office game is played within a company by the employees. These can either use the phone to call *C*, or not *W*, or they can go down to Dexter's Diner to talk, *D*. Now, for the population of employees *P* where conditionalizing is impossible there are two evolutionary stable equilibria. One is that of always going down to Dexter's. The other one consists in using the phone, calling up with prob. ½ and waiting with prob. ½. Is the mixed equilibrium a convention in this game?

Figure 7
The office game:

		Player 2		
		C	W	D
Player 1	C	0,0	4,4	0,0
	W	4,4	0,0	0,0
	D	0,0	0,0	1,1

What would we say if we observed a population having played this game sufficiently many times so as to reach equilibrium? Of those populations always playing (*D, D*) we would probably say that they are following the convention *go to Dexter's*. But this convention would not be relative to that of *call half the time, wait half the time*. Rather it would be relative to the convention of *rely on the phone*, which is done by mixing with equal probabilities between *C* and *W*, the latter of which is *not* a matter of convention. That is, mixing is not part of the convention.

The reason for this subtle difference seems to me to be exactly that pinned out by Lewis. If one of two employees in a given company plays the mixed strategy associated with the mixed equilibrium, the other could do whatever he or she pleases. For instance, he or she could always be calling without this changing the payoffs they receive. Here it would indeed seem strange to say that they were following the convention *call half the time, wait half the time*, but not to say that they *rely on the phone* rather than *go to Dexter's*. Thus, the game they play is rather that in figure 8.

Figure 8
The Office Convention:

		player 2	
		T	C
player 1	Try calling around	**2,2**	0,0
	Cantina	0,0	**1,1**

The simple reason for this use of language is that we *do* want to require with Lewis that by using the term *convention* in referring to a regularity we intend to distinguish the phenomenon referred to from mere regularities by describing it as just one out of multiple available solutions for solving a given coordination problem, dependent in some way on past conformity. And here our use of language is correct as it identifies the conventional aspect; not all kinds of other things such as that we play matching pennies in this universe, play it as a constant-sum game, or use the mixed strategies combining in the mixed equilibrium. Put simpler, a convention is one out of multiple available solutions for solving a given *coordination problem*, and mixing is not part of this problem.

V. Common knowledge and convention

At this point one may reasonably wonder why Lewis would use so much energy on the idea of common knowledge, if it is quite easily showed not to be a necessary condition for convention. Lewis himself made several attempts at defending the common knowledge requirement. It need only be of a 'poor kind', merely 'potential', 'irremediably nonverbal', or even fragmented in the sense knowledge in *sensu diviso* (Lewis 1969, 63; Lewis 1975). However, in none of these senses does common knowledge come to figure as a necessary constitutive or operational feature of conventions.[20] Instead, we may use the above discussion to give an alternative suggestion as to why Lewis may have insisted, incorrectly, that common knowledge is necessary for a convention to operate.

The suggestion made here is that past conformity to a convention, *if made common knowledge*, may help to generate inductive expectations concerning future behaviour of the type necessary for a convention to operate, granted that the *indication* relation is taken to provide some kind of inductive reasons in the way as e.g. sketched by Cubitt and Sugden (2003).

To illustrate what is meant by this, consider the special case where a group G of prisoners of many nationalities arrives in a camp. Each prisoner is isolated in his own cell. It is then announced by speakers in the courtyard that to the enjoyment of the personnel they have to play the Driving game each day, but with deadly payoffs resulting from coordination failure. Finally, it is also announced that "everyone has conformed to R in the past" – call this last announcement the state of affairs A. Now, in this case everyone in G has reason to believe that A holds. Also, A indicates to everyone in G that everyone in G has reason to believe that A holds. But will A indicate to everyone in G (given our assumptions) that p, where p is the proposition, that "everyone will conform to R in the future". Only if R is a *proper* equilibrium, I dare say. If R is a regularity implying play of the mixed equilibrium of the driving game such as "everyone has hitherto conformed to always flipping a coin and gone *left* if heads, and *right* if tails", this will have no effect on expectations. If I believe that everyone else is going to flip a coin in the future I wouldn't care about flipping a coin, since that would have no effect. Likewise, if I thought that you expected me to flip a coin, then I wouldn't expect you to flip a coin. If I thought that you expected me to expect that you flip a coin, I would expect that you wouldn't expect me to flip a coin, and, hence, though you could flip a coin yourself, you would have no particular reason to do so, and definitely not one derived from A. So we wouldn't expect anything from the announcement; the common knowledge of A would indicate no proposition p to us relevant for solving our coordination problem. In this way Lewis' idea of common knowledge may be utilized to identify the conventional aspect of a given practice.

Literature

Aumann, Robert J. (1976), "Agreeing to Disagree", *The Annals of Statistics*, 4, 1236-1239.
Bicchieri, Cristina (2000), "Words and Deeds", in J. Nida-Rümelin and W. Spohn (eds.), *Rationality, Rules, and Structure* (Kluwer Academic Publishers).
Binmore, Ken (1993), *Game Theory and the Social Contract*, Vol. 1, *Playing Fair* (Cambridge, Mass.: MIT Press).
Binmore, Ken (2007), *Game Theory: A Very Short Introduction* (Oxford: Oxford University Press).
Burge, Tyler (1975), "On Knowledge and Convention", *The Philosophical Review*, 84, 249-55.
Cooper, David E. (1977), "Lewis on our Knowledge of Conventions", *Mind*, New Series, 86, 256-61.
Cubitt, Robin and Robert Sugden (2003), "Common Knowledge, Salience and Convention: A Reconstruction of David Lewis's Game Theory", *Economics and Philosophy*, 19, 175-210.
Fudenberg, Drew and David K. Levine (1998), *The Theory of Learning in Games* (Cambridge, Mass.: MIT Press).
Gilbert, Margaret (1981), "Game Theory and Convention", *Synthese*, 46, 41-93.
Gilbert, Margaret (1989), *On Social Facts* (Princeton: Princeton University Press).
Grandy, Richard E. (1977), Review of *Convention: A Philosophical Study* by David K. Lewis, *The Journal of Philosophy*, 74, 129-39.
Hansen, P. G. (2007), "Evolutionary Games and Social Conventions", in A. Pietarinen (ed.), *Game Theory and Linguistic Meaning:*, Current Research in the Semantics/Pragmatics Interface, vol. 18 (Elsevier Science).
Heal, Jane (1978), "Common knowledge", *Philosophical Quarterly*, 28, 116-31.
Jamieson, D. (1975), "David Lewis on Convention", *Canadian Journal of Philosophy*, 5, 73-81.
Lewis, David K. (1969), *Convention: A Philosophical Study* (Cambridge, Mass.: Harvard University Press).
Lewis, David K. (1975), "Languages and Language", *Minnesota Studies in the Philosophy of Science*, vol. VII, University of Minnesota Press, 3-35.
Maynard-Smith, John (1982), *Evolution and the Theory of Games* (Cambridge: Cambridge University Press).
Metha, Judith, Chris Starmer and Robert Sugden (1994a), "Focal Points in Games with Multiple Equilibria: An Experimental Investigation", *Theory and Decision*, 36, 163-85.
Metha, Judith, Chris Starmer and Robert Sugden (1994b), "The Nature of Salience: An Experimental Investigation of Pure Coordination Games", *American Economic Review*, 84, 658-73.
Nash Jr., John F. (1950), "Equilibrium points in N-person games", *Proceedings of the National Academy of Sciences*, 36, 48-49.
Schelling, Thomas C. (1960), *The Strategy of Conflict* (Cambridge, Mass.: Harvard University Press).
Skyrms, Brian (1996), *Evolution of the Social Contract* (Cambridge: Cambridge University Press).
Sugden, Robert (1986), *The Economics of Rights, Co-operation and Welfare* (Oxford: Basil Blackwell).
Sugden, Robert (2001), "The Evolutionary Turn in Game Theory", *Journal of Economic Methodology*, 8, 113-30.
Sugden, Robert (2004), *The Economics of Rights, Co-operation and Welfare*, 2nd and revised ed. (London: Palgrave Macmillan).

Verbeek, Bruno (2002), *Instrumental Rationality and Moral Philosophy: An Essay on the Virtues of Co-Operation* (Kluwer Academic Publishers).
Weibull, Jörgen W. (1995), *Evolutionary Game Theory* (Cambridge Mass.: MIT Press).
Wittgenstein, Ludwig (1953), *Philosophical Investigations* (Oxford: Basil Blackwell).
Young, H. Peyton (1998), *Individual Strategy and Social Structure: An Evolutionary Theory of Institutions* (Princeton, N.J.: Princeton University Press).

Notes

1. I thank Robert Sugden, Ryan Muldoon and Ken Binmore for comments on the argument of this paper.
2. It should be emphasized, though, that Lewis' synthesis of game theory and convention as well as the idea that something like common knowledge was needed to explain coordination was forestalled by Schelling 1960.
3. Throughout this paper I will stay true to Lewis rather than convention and use proper rather than strict in order to avoid any confusion.
4. This second point may not appear as relevant to the question at hand immediately. Yet, it follows from the final argument in this paper, that if the requirement of common knowledge was trivial one could just use this requirement from the outset to exclude mixed equilibria as conventions.
5. In particular, Lewis' intention was to give an analysis of semantic conventions that did not presuppose any conventions itself in terms of language use. Hence his analysis is one of tacit convention.
6. I use the inverted commas since it will turn out that this is only one of multiple conceptions of stability available within a game theoretical framework as well as since what is meant by 'stability' in many analyses is actually quite vague.
7. For one, when the game runs over n stages, the strategy space of the driving game becomes 2^n. Further, some argue that a strategy is not merely defined by the behaviour associated with it, but also its description, see e.g. Verbeek 2002. If this latter claim is accepted, then the strategy space of even a single stage is infinite (see also the next note).
8. Here I am not concerned with the problem that any rule or strategy will always be underdetermined by any finite series of observed action combinations. Instead I will just assume that the players posit strategy sets such as {always left, always right} rather than actions sets such as {left, right} from this point in the paper and on. This, though, does only push the mentioned problem of underdetermination to the level of strategies. Whatever the level, however, the problem of underdetermination is either irrelevant or undermines the theory of convention if paid attention to. Readers are referred to my forthcoming work on common knowledge and Schelling salience in order to see why I find the former scenario to be the case.
9. This is just one of several definitions given by Lewis in Convention. But as these other definitions elaborate on complications not pertaining to our present purpose, I choose the simplest one.
10. This, however, has been challenged by Jamieson 1975, Gilbert 1989, but see also Bicchieri 2000 for a rejoinder.
11. The interpretation offered here dispenses with the requirement that (3) and (5) be common knowledge, since (3) is an idiosyncratic requirement made by Lewis (see next note), while it is obviously absurd that (5) should be required to be common knowledge in P, as pointed out originally by Burge 1975.

12. See, e.g. Gilbert 1981.
13. In fact, Lewis' analysis is not one of common knowledge but rather one of common reason to believe. Reasons to believe are interpreted by Lewis as potential beliefs that players may realize by going through the necessary steps of reasoning.
14. This assumption that the a game is played repeatedly within a population of agents randomly drawn and perhaps also randomly assigned to a player position makes for distinguishing between 'agents' and 'players' in the rest of the paper.
15. See the different convergence results in Fudenberg and Levine 1998.
16. Thanks to Ken Binmore who pointed out to me in personal communication that this well-known equilibrium was one of 'coordination'.
17. See note 7 above.
18. Here we stay true to the earlier assumption that the only strategies available even in the repeated game are left, right and any mixed strategy that has these as support.
19. In the following, knowledge of a series of results within evolutionary game theory are presupposed. The uninitiated reader is referred to Weibull 1995 and Hansen 2007.
20. See e.g. the first part of the discussion by Cooper 1977 showing this. The second part of this discussion insisting on common knowledge as part of any convention is, however, undermined by the earlier argument against this requirement.

DEONTOLOGY – BORN AND KEPT IN SERVITUDE BY UTILITARIANISM[1]

Asger Sørensen

Department of Philosophy of Education, School of Education, University of Aarhus, Denmark

ABSTRACT. The distinction between teleology and deontology is today almost universally accepted within practical philosophy, but deontology is and has from the beginning been subordinate to utilitarianism. 'Deontology' was constructed by Bentham to signify the art and science of private morality within a utilitarian worldview. The classical distinction was constructed by Broad as a refinement of Sidgwick's utilitarianism, and then adopted by Frankena. To Broad it signified two opposite tendencies in ethics, in Frankena's textbooks, however, it becomes an exclusive distinction, where deontology signifies disregard for consequences, and it is therefore almost impossible to think of deontology as a framework for a comprehensive ethical theory. This conception, however, is adopted by Rawls, and in his contractarian interpretation of deontology it is in fact no more within the sphere of ethics.

Introduction

One of the most generally acknowledged distinctions in ethics is the distinction between deontology and teleology. The concept of deontology plays a crucial role in analyses and discussions not just in ethics, but also in political philosophy, philosophy of law and various sciences. Nevertheless, very few scholars have given the concept of deontology the close attention that such prominence should merit. This article will contribute to filling out this gap by arguing that the widespread understanding of deontology as formally opposed to – and thus, in a sense equal to – teleology or consequentialism is not just incomplete, but actually misleading. Through an analysis of different conceptions of 'deontology', I will argue that deontology as a category is and has always been subordinate to a utilitarian frame of mind; therefore, opponents of utilitarianism or consequentialism like John Rawls should not identify themselves as deontologists. The main figures in this analysis are Bentham, Broad and Frankena, but neither my claim nor my arguments are primarily historical. Before venturing into the main part of my analysis, I will therefore elaborate on the systematic perspective.

In mainstream practical philosophy it is widely accepted that the roots of the modern concept of deontology are found in Broad's distinction between deontology and teleology in his book *Five Types of Ethical Theory* (1930). From its origins as a relatively esoteric analytical term in pre-war Anglo-Saxon ethics, 'deontology' became institutionalized as an important ethical category in the textbooks of P.H. Nowell-Smith (1954) and William K. Frankena (1963 and 1974). Since these publications deontological theories have been considered to be opposed to teleological theories in Anglophone ethics, the standard example of the former being the ethics of Kant (cf. e.g. Nowell-Smith 1954, 134; Frankena 1963, 25; Hallgarth 1998, 610), whereas the latter usually is exemplified by some kind of utilitarianism. 'Deontology' in this sense was the point of departure for the political philosophy of Rawls (1971/99, 26), and it was also in this sense understood on the continent by Jürgen Habermas (cf. e.g. 1991, 168).

However, a brief survey of 'deontology' in non-Anglophone philosophical encyclopedias and dictionaries (cf. e.g. Ferrater Mora 1994, 816; Lalande 1991, 816; Canto-Sperber 1996, 401; Ritter 1972, 114) reveals an older, more basic conception of 'deontology', which is derived from the Greek words '*to deon*' and '*logos*'. The latter should not cause us any trouble, and the former can be translated as "that which is proper" or "what ought to be". As a first approach to the meaning of 'deontology' it therefore seems reasonable to define it as "the teachings or science of what is proper and what ought to be", in short, "the science of duty". This conception can be encountered in modern ethics, especially on the continent, as demonstrated by the dictionaries just mentioned, but also in the Anglophone world (cf. e.g. Muirhead 1940, Carmichael 1949, Campbell Garnett 1956 and Nowell-Smith 1954, 185).

What is even more surprising, however, is that the man who constructed the neo-logism 'deontology' apparently was the same one, who invented utilitarianism, namely Bentham himself. Bentham even left an unfinished manuscript, which was published in 1834, with the title *Deontology*, which was thought to complete utilitarianism as a general worldview. The manuscript stated, for the first and only time, the specifics of Bentham's utilitarianism as moral philosophy.[2] For Bentham, 'deontology' was therefore not at all intended to be opposed to utilitarianism; quite the contrary.

Originally, deontology was constructed as a part of utilitarianism; today they are seen as opposed. What shall we make out of this shift? Is it just a curious fact, which shows the contingency of semantical meaning and the irony of history?[3] Or can it give us a hint of something more substantial? I will argue that this curious historical fact about deontology does indeed express something of substantial conceptual interest, namely that in the distinction between deontology and teleology, deontology is and has always been the subordinate and relatively less important aspect. From the very beginning, the meaning of 'deontology' has been tied to that of 'utilitarianism' and this is still the case, although both the meaning of utilitarianism, of deontology and the content of the relation between the two terms have changed.

Considering the teleological aspect, utilitarianism has been criticised by moralists ever since its conception more than 200 years ago (Schneewind 1977, 128-30), but nevertheless it has dominated Anglophone ethics for decades (Schneewind 1993, 155). Today it seems more fitting than ever, and this is reflected in the development of the vocabulary used in textbooks and academic discussions. In accordance with its etymological roots (*telos* = 'goal' or 'end'), teleological ethics is taken to stress the importance of the end in moral action and ethical theory. From this perspective, utilitarianism can be grouped together with the ethics of Aristotle (cf. Edel 1973, 175), and this is also how Rawls considers it (1971/99, 22, 35). As the standard counter-position of 'deontology', however, the traditional category 'teleology' is today in most cases replaced by the term 'consequentialism' (cf. e.g. Stegmüller 1989, 227), a term, which is even more closely related to utilitarianism than is teleology. Using 'consequentialism' implies a direct identification of the general ethical category with the utilitarian scheme of thought, since utilitarians explicitly state that only the consequences of an action – in the classical view, the resulting happiness – should count as reasons to decide whether an action is dutiful or not.[4]

This terminological development is also reflected in the other aspect of the distinction, where 'deontology' nowadays often is substituted by 'non-consequentialism', indicating – sometimes explicitly – that it is hard to give deontology a positive meaning, and therefore that it is best understood in contrast to consequentialism (Davis 1993, 206). Furthermore, one can point to the common understanding of deontology in terms like 'agent-relativity' (cf. e.g. Ellis 1992, 856), 'deontological constraints' (e.g. Nagel 1986; Kymlicka 1988, 180), or 'agent-centred restrictions' (e.g. Scheffler 1984; Brook 1991, 190), which all tend to reduce deontology to a set of exceptions, which must be taken into account by ethics, but which cannot be understood in a sufficiently coherent way to constitute in itself a theoretical approach to philosophical ethics.

I will argue that from the days of Bentham until today, the structural position of deontology in relation to utilitarianism has remained the same, even though the referential content of the two terms has changed. This way of construing the relation reflects a more general point, which is central to the argument of this article. Every word is one aspect of one or more distinctions, and every distinction has two or more aspects, which are relative to each other. A distinction is, however, not just given. It is always the answer to a specific concern and therefore expresses a special point of view. This makes it possible to question the universal validity – or applicability – of a distinction, even when it is almost universally accepted, as it has been shown by American pragmatists in relation to analytical distinctions like *a priori/a posteriori* (cf. C. I. Lewis), and analytic/synthetic (cf. Quine).

I will, however, go one step further and follow Derrida in claiming that since every distinction has a special point of view, it both has a focus of attention and a horizon, a centre and a periphery (cf. e.g. Derrida 1968, 128). As such it is not only contingent, but it is also basically asymmetrical, and the revelation of the hierarchical pattern is at the same time an exposure of the preconditions, which make the distinction meaningful. Consequently, a distinction can be seen as an expression of a relation of power. In the distinction in question, I will claim that deontology plays the subordinate part, conceived within and still dominated by the utilitarian scheme of thought.[5]

This argument becomes important when the intention is to formulate alternatives to utilitarianism within practical philosophy. Expressing this resistance in terms of a positive identification with deontology – as done by Rawls – is to stay within a conceptual framework defined by utilitarianism. No matter how good one's intentions, or how excellent one's terminological skills and moral insight may be, identifying positively with deontology makes it almost impossible to counter the utilitarian programme and its domination in ethics.

In this article, developing on an earlier suggestion (Sørensen 2003, 42-49), I analyze three classical concepts of deontology from the perspective sketched above. First, I present Bentham's original concept of deontology, which is closely connected to utilitarianism (1). Second, as the main part, I analyse the classical teleology-deontology distinction as conceived of by Broad (2), and developed by Frankena (3), where deontology as the disregard of consequences is considered irrational in relation to an overall conception of ethics determined by teleology and utilitarianism. Finally, I present the distinction in the form which is accepted by Rawls in *A Theory of Justice*, and how it makes egoism the basis of his deontological political philosophy (4).

Even though my approach is not historical, I will present the main conceptions of deontology in chronological order. However, I will not investigate the historical transformations of the concept, but focus on each particular conception of deontology, in order to demonstrate the specifics of each particular subordination to utilitarianism.

1. Bentham

The foundation on which Bentham constructed the neo-logism 'deontology' was the Greek words mentioned above, and its basic meaning is the 'science of duty'. This meaning is in accordance with what Bentham himself writes in his pedagogical treatise *Chrestomathia* from 1817, where 'deontology' is defined as

> an account or an indication of that which, on the occasion in question, whatsoever it be, is – (i.e. by him who speaks or writes is regarded as being) – *fit, fitting, becoming, proper*. (Goldworth 1983, xx)

This definition (which is one of the few examples of Bentham's use of the term in texts printed while he was still alive) can be understood as containing both a theoretical and a practical aspect in the Aristotelian sense of the words. Giving an 'account' can be merely theoretical; but 'indicating' what one considers to be proper in a particular situation is at the same time an evaluation or a recommendation, and as such an 'indication' is always practical, i.e. ethical or political.

Accordingly, the *Deontology* is divided in two parts, an "exegetical", "expository" part, normally called the theoretical part and a more "practical part".[6] Both parts, however, are meant to be conducive to the "ultimate and practical result" of "this work", which is

> the pointing out to each man on each occasion what course of conduct promises to be in the highest degree conducive to his happiness: to his own happiness, first and last; to the happiness of others, no farther than in so far as his happiness is promoted by promoting theirs, than his interest coincides with theirs. (*Deont.*, 123)

The theoretical part relates virtues and vices to happiness or "well-being" (*Deont.*, 130), as Bentham prefers to call it here. Virtues and vices are "fictitious entities, imagined and spoken of as real for the purpose of discourse", without which, however, "discourse on subjects such as this could not be carried on" (*Deont.*, 126). Accordingly, Bentham wants to explain virtues and vices in terms of the only real entities, pleasure and pain. Hence, he will show that all virtues can be seen as "modifications of two all comprehensive ones", "prudence and benevolence".

In accordance with the overall goal of the *Deontology*, the practical part is first of all about "dictates of purely self-regarding prudence". However, because the conduct of oneself affects the well-being of others, it is necessary both to consider the "dictates of benevolence" and the "dictates of extra-regarding prudence" (*Deont.*, 122-24). The second part is therefore divided into these three subdivisions.

Seen as an art, the purpose of deontology is to promote "human welfare". The distinction between self-regarding and extra-regarding prudence, therefore, becomes a distinction between "self-regarding deontology", which aims to promote the welfare of the actor in question, and "extra-regarding deontology", which aims to promote the welfare of "all persons concerned other than the individual agent" (*Deont.*, 198).

Bentham apparently considers deontology to be primarily concerned with one's own happiness, especially in one's private life; but this does not mean – or is not intended to mean – that one should be self-centred in a selfish way. The individual achievement of particular pleasures is only a "means" in respect to the general end, i.e. mere "subordinate ends" (*Deont.*, 125). Among these particular pleasures are those stemming from sympathy, and they include the genuine pleasure of knowing that others fare well. The "business of the deontologist" (*Deont.*, 193) is precisely to "bring to view these comparatively latent ties" (*Deont.*, 195) between self-regarding and extra-regarding interests, and to show their "points of coincidence" (*Deont.*, 193).

The purpose of the *Deontology* is to persuade the readers to accept the basic principles of utilitarianism, and then to offer guidelines for how to act correctly as a utilitarian in private life – "morality made easy" (*Deont.* 119), as Bentham writes on the drafts for the title page. However, if we consider the concept of 'deontology' as such – as distinguished from the work called *Deontology* – it has a more "general end", which is:

> the same end or object which not only every branch of art or science has, but every human thought as well as every human action has – and not only has but ought to have: the giving increase in some shape or other to man's well-being – say in one word the sum of human happiness. (*Deont.*, 125)

In so far as man's conduct is conducive to this end, it is to be called 'virtuous'; 'virtue' is then a 'characteristic' of man, which is manifested by "his conduct, his actions, his deportment". 'Vicious' and 'vice' are not surprisingly defined as the opposite of 'virtuous' and 'virtue' (*Deont.*, 125). Deontology, therefore, must have as its goal the promotion of virtuous acts and virtues as such, and with such a goal, deontology has to take obligations into account. Basically obligations are also considered "a species of fictious entity", but nevertheless the 'business' of deontology includes:

> the distribution of obligations, [...] marking in the field of action the spots upon which it is proper that obligation in one shape or another should consider itself as attaching; and, in the case of a conflict between obligations issuing from different sources, in determining which should obtain and which should yield the preference. (*Deont.*, 171)

Understanding the ends of deontology as such, Bentham considers it a

> branch of the art and science which has for its object the learning and shewing for the information of each individual, by what means the net amount of his happiness may be made as large as possible; of each in so far as it is dependent on his own conduct: the happiness of each individual separately being considered, and thereby that of every individual among those whose happiness on this occasion an object of regard (*Deont.*, 124-25).

Deontology is in general described as a branch "of the art and science of Eudaemonics", and at the same time 'deontology' is the same as "Ethics (taken in the largest sense of the word)" (*Deont.*, 124-25). Deontology is, we must conclude, ethics at large, and as such it is a branch of the science and art of eudaemonics.

A deontologist, then, apparently does not have to be utilitarian. In Bentham's terms, he can also be ascetic, or 'ipsedixital', i.e. basing his indication on an 'opinion', without reference to "happiness or unhappiness" (*Util.*, 304-05). The term 'deontology' is not meant to be exclusively utilitarian. Other worldviews can have their deontologies as well. As such, deontology is something relatively limited, i.e. just a part of an all-inclusive faith such as utilitarianism.

'Deontology' in this sense apparently refers to the teaching of private morality, that is, of duties that can be deduced from the general principles. In other words, deontology cannot be defined substantially on its own terms; its content can only be deduced from already accepted general principles. In this case, there is nothing that conceals that deontology is dominated by something else; deontology is simply defined as a sub-category, the teachings of duties consistent with an already accepted worldview.

*

In sum, Bentham apparently has at least two conceptions of deontology. The first conception takes deontology – as art and science, or art with science attached – as the most comprehensive category, divided into private deontology, which is private morality, and public deontology, which includes legislation and government in general. This conception is consistent both with the remark that considers deontology as ethics in general, i.e. practical philosophy, and with the specification of deontology as a subcategory of a more comprehensive worldview.[7]

The second conception takes eudaemonics – again, as arts and sciences, or arts only – to be the most comprehensive category, and it comprises deontology, understood as private morality, politics, legislation, and government, all on the same footing. If deontology is ethics in this sense, then ethics is concerned with private morality, but pre-defined as eudaemonic, as an activity aiming at one specific *telos*, namely happiness. As such, deontology is a subcategory within a teleological framework, *in casu* utilitarianism.

The first conception of deontology is apparently relatively neutral towards the utilitarian scheme of thought, but since it is only a formal conception, it must get its content from the worldview of which it is a part. Consequently, when Bentham defines the content of deontology, it is utilitarian. The second conception of deontology adds to this point. It shows that Bentham considers ethics as such to be inherently teleological, and that makes deontology subordinate to this scheme of thought as well.

2. Broad

Both of Bentham's conceptions of 'deontology' are consistent with the general understanding of deontology as the science of duties. As mentioned above, however, when it comes to the modern philosophical sense of 'deontology', one normally refers to Broad's *Five Types of Ethical Theory* (*F.T.*). Here the term deontology is introduced without any reference to Bentham in a specific context, namely the analysis of the Sidgwick's *Method of Ethics*. Broad wants to qualify the applications of 'ought' in judgements, and the distinctions between deontological, teleological and logical are offered as such qualifications.

To Broad, the deontological use of 'ought' in a judgement means that an action should be performed in a certain type of situation, "regardless of the goodness or badness of the probable consequences" (*F.T.*, 162). Broad notes that many people would deny that they ever make such 'unconditional' judgements, but they can probably be seen as making statements which employ 'ought' teleologically, meaning "that everyone ought to aim at certain ends without any ulterior motive, *e.g.* his own greatest happiness, at the greatest happiness of all sentient being, and so on." At last, 'ought' can be applied logically, meaning that if someone considers a certain end to be ultimate, "then he *ought* to be consistent about it" (*F.T.*, 162).

Broad considers whether these three applications of 'ought' also involve three different meanings. He distinguishes between the narrow sense of 'ought', applied to actions "which an agent could do if he willed" (*F.T.*, 161), and the wider sense, where this condition does not apply. According to Broad, the wide sense is involved in the teleological application of 'ought', and the narrow, in the logical application. "For we believe it is within the powers of any sane human being to be consistent if he tries." However, "the logical ought is just a special case of the deontological ought" (*F.T.*, 163), and this relation is important, because the narrow sense of ought is made acceptable to those who do not acknowledge the deontological application of 'ought' in general.

Broad ends up with the classical binary distinction between teleology and deontology. What is interesting, however, is that the logical and thus deontological use of ought is based on the idea of consistency in *action* and not in relation to *propositions*. Apparently, Broad thinks that 'consistent' means that one ought to choose the appropriate means to realize an end, and to avoid actions "inconsistent with its realisation" (*F.T.*, 163). With this concept of consistency, however, it seems strange to subsume the logical meaning of 'ought' under the deontological, since it is teleology which by definition should be focused on actions as a means to an end, and not deontology, which is more preoccupied with the actions in themselves.

To make this point more clearly, one can employ Weber's famous distinction between means-end rationality, often called instrumental rationality, and value-rationality. Means-end rationality is the kind of rationality that is employed by economic theory and rational choice theory, where what matters is the right choice of means in view of the optimal realization of given ends (Weber 1921-22, 12). The rationality involved in value-rationality is rationality in another sense, i.e. the kind of rationality employed in logical reasoning, e.g. in the deduction from premises to a valid conclusion. To Weber, it is this latter kind of rationality that can be attributed to the protestant 'ethics of intention', which like deontology is defined by its disregard for consequences (Weber 1919, 551). An ethics of intention is rational and consistent in the strictly logical sense that its particular judgement can be deduced from one or more general principles and that it is therefore non-contradictory.

One would think that it was consistency and rationality in this latter sense, i.e. the rationality involved in making non-contradictory judgements, that must be involved, if the logical sense of 'ought' is to be subsumed under deontology. And it would be tempting to interpret Broad's distinction between a wider and a narrower sense of 'ought' as the distinction between a weak and a strong sense, i.e. as the distinction between what one ought to do in relation to given ends – e.g. one ought to love one's neighbours – and what one ought to do in relation to logical constraints – that one ought not to contradict oneself. Especially since Broad does think of rationality in this way, when he interprets Kant (*F.T.*, 128).

But in his analysis of Sidgwick's utilitarianism, Broad uses the concept of means-end rationality in his notion of consistency, although both he and Sidgwick (in contrast to Weber) are aware that rationality in the sense of "hypothetical imperatives" (*F.T.*, 152) can be employed both in an egoistic way and in a universal or utilitarian way. Even though consistency is a fair demand to the deontological and logical use of 'ought', neither Broad's logical application of 'ought', nor his conception of deontology has anything to do with logic in a strict sense. The difference between these two conceptions of rationality becomes even more important with Rawls' idea of himself as an deontologist, as we shall see below.

*

It is this distinction concerning the application and meaning of 'ought' that Broads generalizes to divide ethical theory into two classes. Deontological theories contain propositions of the form "Such and such a kind of action would always be right (or wrong) in such and such circumstances, no matter what the consequences might be." Teleological theories judge the rightness or wrongness of an action by its "tendency to produce certain consequences which are intrinsically good or bad" (*F.T.*, 206-07). Broad thinks that both types of theories can be found in monistic and in pluralistic versions, and that teleological theories can be divided into egoistic and non-egoistic types, with utilitarianism being an example of the latter.

Broad considers this classification to be clearer than Sidgwick's, which distinguishes between intuitionism, egoistic hedonism and utilitarianism, since his own classification is independent of epistemological considerations. From a logical point of view, he is no doubt correct.[8] However, one can ask why deontological theories cannot be either egoistic or non-egoistic. Is being egoistical regardless of the consequences not an option for ethical theory?

The hidden premise that rules out this idea as senseless seems to be that morality, and hence ethics, must be good for something, if not for the individual then for society or humanity in general. And deontological egoism does not seem to be good for anything, neither for oneself nor for anybody else. Keeping in mind Broad's concept of consistency and the concept of rationality implied by it, ethics appears then as a whole to be teleological, which means that the two aspects of the distinction in question cannot be of equal value.

This conclusion is supported by the way Broad analyses Sidgwick's intuitionism in relation to deontology. Trying to make sense of deontology, Broad understands it as claiming that in order to determine the rightness of an actions it is sufficient to consider "*one or a few* characteristics of its *immediate* consequences", treating as irrelevant "the more remote consequences and the other characteristics of the consequences" (*F.T.*, 214). It is claims about the necessary connection between certain kinds of actions and their immediate consequences that Broad finds characteristic of deontology, and those claims are considered to be '*a priori*' judgements.

According to Broad, the difference between teleology and deontology is that the former makes empirically based judgements about the relative non-moral goodness of all of the consequences of an action, whereas the latter makes *a priori* judgements about the connection between some kinds of actions and their immediate moral consequences. Both types of judgement are based on consequences, but teleology makes more comprehensive, empirically based and – from Broad's perspective – therefore better judgements. From a deontological point of view, Broad's concession to utilitarian ethics appears inconsistent (Campell Garnett 1941, 421). Broad's perspective, however, is teleological, at least in his analysis of Sidgwick, and, as Schneewind remarks, the idea that an "action can only be right because it produces good" is "deeply rooted" (Schneewind 1993, 150) in ethics.

Weber made it perfectly clear that in the perspective of calculating means-end rationality, deductive value-rationality was not rational (Weber 1921-22, 13). Not so with Broad. His conception of ethics is not made explicit, but the result is the same. Like the ethics of intention, deontology cannot be understood as rational in the full sense, but appears to be a dogmatic, deficient mode of teleology. Since ethics as such has to be teleological and rationally consistent with regard to means-end, deontology is not an option. In the end, deontology can only be an exception, a category which attracts irrational moralists, fanatics and the like. It is not possible to form a rational ethical theory on this basis.

This bias in favour of teleology, however, should not come as a surprise, since the distinction between deontology and teleology is based on Sidgwick's tri-partition of ethics in intuitionism, egoistic hedonism, and universal hedonism. The distinction thus reflects what utilitarians themselves often consider the main opposition to utilitarianism, egoism and intuitionism, i.e. those who are selfish and those who on moral grounds oppose the rational calculation of means and ends, i.e. those whom Bentham called "ipse-dixits". Broad states in the beginning of *Five Types* that he has chosen 'men of genius whose views differ from each other as much as possible' (*F.T.*, 1). The distinction between teleology and deontology, however, only appears in the final analysis of Sidgwick, not in relation to the four preceding theories, those of Spinoza, Butler, Hume and Kant. Kant is considered a deontologist (*F.T.*, 207), but only within Sidgwick's utilitarian classification of ethical theories.

Broad's distinction is clearly an improvement on Sidgwick's. Through "a slight shift in terminology" he clarifies "what is inherent in Sidgwicks position", adding only a slight "modification", but resting on "the same essential principles" (Salzman 1995, 76-78). In Derrida's terminology, one could consider Broad's reading of Sidgwick a "displacement" (cf. e.g. Derrida 1967, 29). It is an improvement from a logical point of view, but Broad's new concept of deontology is still conceived within the utilitarian scheme of thought, although differently than in Bentham's original conception.

*

The relation between the terms, however, is even more complex than suggested by the analysis so far. Broad states that "*purely* deontological and *purely* teleological theories are rather ideal limits than real existents" (*F.T.*, 207), and even that "neither concept might be definable in terms of the other" (*F.T.*, 278). This way of employing the distinction shows the bi-partition to be less a classification of theories than an analytical distinction, which is used to clarify two aspects, which Broad considers to be inherent in almost every ethical theory: the teleological focus on the ends and consequences of an action; and the deontological focus on what is considered to be intrinsically right. And in this latter context, Broad does not mention the disregard for the consequences of an action performed in accordance with such an ideal.

Teleology and deontology can be understood as two almost independent – or to employ Weber's terminology, "ideal-typical" (cf. Weber 1904, 190-92) – aspects of ethical theory. "Most actual theories are mixed, some being predominantly deontological and others predominantly teleological". To Broad, Sidgwick's utilitarianism is an example of an "almost purely teleological theory", but even in such a theory there is something considered "*intrinsically* right", namely a "mode of distribution", and "to this extent Sidgwick's theory must be counted as deontological" (*F.T.* 207-08).[9]

Broad develops this conception of the distinction in more detail. In general, he characterizes teleology as "an empirical or inductive theory", taking probable tendencies in the overall consequences into consideration. Deontology is claiming *a priori* rightness or wrongness in such judgements, whereas a teleologist demands empirical evidence. But since the distinction is to be understood as analytical, Broad's general point is that "every Teleological theory does involve at least one *a priori* judgement", namely one that "expresses a necessary connection between a certain non-ethical characteristic and the ethical characteristic of goodness" (*F.T.*, 213-14).

Deontology becomes in this sense the *a priori* aspects of an ethical theory, including not only the *a priori* claims that some actions or modes of actions are unconditionally right, but also that some things are intrinsically good. Sidgwick, even though a hedonist, "is not a pure teleologist, since his six ethical intuitions are deontological propositions" (*F.T.*, 228).

This conception of the distinction between deontology and teleology is epistemological. Hence, the distinction can no longer be considered merely a classification of theories operating within the limits of normative ethics. By changing the criteria of distinction from the significance of ends and consequences to the question of *a priori* versus empirical evidence, the distinction becomes meta-ethical. Broad tried to escape the epistemological premises inherent in Sidgwick's classification by an analytical clarification. But epistemology seems to have sneaked in again, behind his back, so to speak![10]

Since the distinction is normative in one sense and meta-ethical in another, all kinds of utilitarian ethics can be labelled as deontological, at least to a certain extent. This conception of the distinction, however, makes it possible to give sense to the logically constructed idea of egoistic deontological theories. Consider for example those ethical theories that hold freedom as the ultimate value, based on an idea of a moral sense and on a firm belief in the invisible hand or the equilibrium theory of neo-classical economy. To a non-believer, they often seem to regard the freedom expressed in rational market-behaviour as intrinsically right, as *a priori* valuable, disregarding empirical evidence showing the obvious inhuman consequences of the free market in society at large.

Such ethical theories could, with this extension of Broad's terminology, be called predominantly deontological in both the meta-ethical and the normative sense to the extent that they consider egoism – sometimes disguised under the term 'prudence' – as intrinsically right, no matter what the consequences might be. In contrast, such ethicists would be predominantly teleological in the normative sense, to the extent that they justify egoism by an end like the wealth of nations or the universal happiness of mankind. However, they would be teleological in both senses only to the extent that they actually would be capable of being proven wrong by empirical evidence. And this happens very rarely in matters of politics and ethics, since practical philosophy not only acknowledges reality, but also ideal – i.e. non-real – matters.

Even though deontology is inherent in most actual ethical theories, it is clear that deontology as such cannot be regarded as a rational ethical position, as conceived of by Broad. The empiricism and means-end rationality implicit in teleology, as well as the concept of consistency as choosing the right means to a given end, does not admit of any good reasons for adopting a pure deontological approach, either in the normative or in the meta-ethical sense. Because of the teleological conception of ethics inherent in Broad's analysis of Sidgwick, deontology simply refers to the unconditional, dogmatic and hence non-justified and irrational aspect of morality, which, however, must be accounted for by any comprehensive ethical theory.

3. Frankena

Broad made substantial contributions to the clarification of Sidgwicks utilitarianism and made the line of thinking behind his own distinction very clear. The distinction is today well established in practical philosophy in Broad's original wording thanks to Nowell-Smith and especially Frankena, whose textbooks from the 1960s and 1970s became a widely used references within Anglophone ethics.[11] And Anglophone ethics was all there was in these two decades, while the continental mainstream formulated normative matters in terms of politics. Textbooks – it is usually thought – must be simple and unambiguous. And what Frankena does is to remove all possibilities of confusion in Broad's distinction, and place it firmly within a general conception of ethics structured by teleology.

Broad's last word in *Five Types* was a warning against the "danger of oversimplification" (*F.T.*, 284) in ethics. In Frankena's textbooks oversimplification is not considered to be a danger at all; quite the contrary, it is understood as the goal to be achieved. Even though the resulting account of ethics is rather strange, it has one great advantage. One does not have to interpret the text as closely as is the case for Bentham's and Broad's texts. When the basic definitions and the overall structure are grasped, then the rest of the content can almost be deduced logically. The problem, however, is that the readers – i.e., students – not only might take this simple picture as the whole truth, but also – and this is much worse – take logical simplification and rigid classification as all there is to thinking about matters of morality and ethics. And this is, I would claim, to a great extent what has happened to ethics in the Anglophone world.

*

The general framework of Frankena's textbooks is the well-known tripartite division of ethics into "three kinds of thinking which relate to morality" (Frankena 1963, 4) in different ways, namely descriptive inquiry, normative judgements and meta-ethical thinking. But the structure of the books also reflects a teleological conception of ethics. Two chapters are dedicated to a normative "theory of obligation" (Frankena 1963, 10): the first to egoism and deontology, the second to teleology, *in casu* utilitarianism. According to the teleological scheme of thought as exposed by Sidgwick et al., a theory of obligation, of what is right to do, must be supplemented by a theory of value, of what is good.

Frankena writes, "a utilitarian must accept some particular theory of value" (Frankena 1963, 15). When Broad's teleologically framed distinction is employed within normative ethics, it is then not so much a question of regarding or disregarding consequences, as of which kind of consequences should be weighed, the moral or the non-moral. Accordingly, there is one chapter about moral value and one about non-moral value, the latter being the ground on which teleological ethics bases its judgements. The final chapter of the book is dedicated solely to meta-ethical questions.

Within this overall teleological structure, a teleological theory is defined as providing the "ultimate criterion or standard of what is morally right, wrong, obligatory etc. [...] the non-moral value that is brought into being". Frankena argues that the justification for this definition is logical, since it would be 'circular' to let the moral value of something depend on "the moral value it promotes" (Frankena 1963, 13). This formally strong argument for basing moral judgement on something non-moral is on its own premises hard to counter, but that is exactly what deontology is supposed to do, since deontological theories are negatively defined to "deny what teleological theories affirm" (Frankena 1963, 14).

The definition of deontology is then deduced logically by negating the statements defining teleology, i.e. by denying that that the non-moral value brought into being is the *only* criterion of moral value. This implies either that there are one or more criteria for what is right to do besides the one proposed by teleology, or that there are one or more completely different criteria. The deontologist can judge an action "right or obligatory simply because of some other fact about it or because of its own nature" and "may adopt any kind of view about what is good or bad in the non-moral sense" (Frankena 1963, 14). This negative definition of 'deontology' leaves no doubt about which side of the distinction is the centre and which is peripheral. It is like dividing the world into fish and non-fish, the latter category being everything in the world, which is not a fish.

It is important to bear in mind that the premises of the general teleological conception of ethics, i.e. means-end rationality and empiricism, have direct implications for the conception of normative ethics. The point of departure for normative ethics is a situation where somebody is to do something of moral relevance, but does not know what to do. It is the teleological perspective as conceived by Broad that defines normative ethics to be about what one ought to do in a specific and particular sense rather than how one ought to live. The primary matter of moral importance becomes the act, not life as a whole.[12] In principle, every single act in a life can be right, and for Frankena this can be the case if we are guided by the right ethical theory. In the attempt to find a non-circular, empirically based and means-end rational justification for what is right to do, the non-moral consequence of the act becomes relevant.

As paradigmatic of what ethics is all about, Frankena analyses Socrates' situation the night before his execution, considering whether to flee or to stay. Behind Socrates' reasoning in the *Crito*, he finds the following ideal:

> (1) We must not let our decision be affected by our emotions, but must examine the question and follow the best reasoning. We must try to get our facts straight and to keep our minds clear. Questions like this can and should be settled by reason.

> (2) We cannot answer such questions by appealing to what people generally think. They may be wrong. We must try to find an answer we ourselves can regard as correct. We must think for ourselves.

> (3) We ought never to do what is morally wrong. The only question we need answer is whether what is proposed is right or wrong, not what will happen to us, what people will think of us, or how we feel about what has happened. (Frankena 1963, 1-2)

In Frankena's view, however, ethics is not directly concerned with solving particular problems in specific situations. But indirectly that is what ethics aims at all the time. Any ethical theory is assumed to presuppose this model of an agent in a situation confronted with a specific problem. As Frankena formulates it, ethics is primarily thought to "provide the general outlines of a normative theory to help us in answering problems about what is right, or ought to be done" (Frankena 1963, 5). In short, ethics is primarily normative ethics.

*

Summarizing the point above, I argue that 'deontology' is defined as 'non-teleology', but within a teleological conception of ethics in general and of normative ethics in particular. This being the case, even though 'deontology' is negatively and thus in principle very broadly defined, in reality, because of the general teleological framework, the possibilities of giving 'deontology' a positive meaning are very limited, as is obvious from Frankena's attempt to do so.

Like Sidgwick and Broad, Frankena's basic distinction within teleology is between egoism and universalism, i.e. utilitarianism. Considering deontology, however, even though Frankena appears to be much stricter in his classificatory logic than his predecessors, this distinction is again avoided. Instead, we are presented with the distinction between act-deontological and rule-deontological theories (Frankena 1963, 14-15). Shifting back to teleology again, one would expect to find a distinction between act-teleological and rule-teleological theories, but instead we find act-utilitarianism confronting rule-utilitarianism (Frankena 1963, 30), that is, a distinction at one level below. How can that be?

The explanation for the confusion of levels of classification is, I will argue, found in the implicit teleological framework, or to be more precise, the inherent utilitarianism in the classificatory logic. Rule-utilitarianism is the well-known answer to one of the most basic critiques of classical utilitarianism, namely that it seems very impractical to have to calculate the balance of good over evil for all foreseeable consequences every time we are to do something. The utilitarian answer is that, if this is really the case, then we must act according to some rules of conduct, and those rules must in turn be justified in the way specified. Hence we can distinguish between act-utilitarians and rule-utilitarians. The two aspects of this distinction, however, are not equal. Act-utilitarianism is the problem, while rule-utilitarianism is the solution.

With this background in mind, it is no wonder that things get a little complicated when this utilitarian sub-distinction is transferred to classify various kinds of deontological theories, i.e. ethical theories that are defined as non-utilitarian. For Frankena, ethics is teleological in the sense defined above and therefore focuses on acts and consequences. This means that both teleology and deontology can only be understood in relation to acts and consequences. This is not a problem for those theories that are already teleological, i.e. utilitarians of various sorts. But for those completely different kinds of ethical thinking, which have to be classified as deontological, since Frankena's exclusive conception of the distinction does not admit of any third possibility, the result is rather bizarre. Act-deontological theories are ethical theories which state that "basic judgements of obligation are all purely particular" and that

> we can and must see or somehow decide separately in each particular situation what is the right or obligatory thing to do, without appealing to any rules. (Frankena 1963, 15)

And this approach means that the ethics of Aristotle is categorized as act-deontological because of his remark that "the decision rests with perception" (Frankena 1963, 15).[13]

Frankena's generalization of the distinction opens up for the transition from teleology to consequentialism. Broad himself, however, also contributed to both of the revisions just mentioned: He dropped the use of the term 'deontology' (cf. Salzman 1995, 101) and later preferred to distinguish between teleology and non-teleology (cf. Broad 1985, 229);[14] and he distinguished between hedonism as a theory of good and evil, i.e. a value theory, and utilitarianism as a theory of right and wrong (cf. Broad 1985, 196), which is exactly the conception of utilitarianism from which the term 'consequentialism' is derived. What is only implicit by Broad, however, is made explicit by Frankena in the structure of his textbooks. For Frankena, deontology is simply non-teleology, and teleology is defined exclusively in terms of consequences. Taken together, this position makes deontology identical to non-consequentialism; and this is indeed the most common understanding of deontology in ethics today.[15]

4. Rawls

It is obvious, however, that apart from the logically very strict construction of deontology, Frankena had serious problems positively specifying what a viable deontological theory could be. In spite of this, a theory of major importance, explicitly referring to Frankena's classification, voluntarily takes this burden upon itself. In *A Theory of Justice*, Rawls states that his "justice as fairness" view is not a utilitarian theory, and that it as non-teleological therefore, "by definition" (1971/99, 26), is a deontological theory. Rawls takes an explicit stand for deontology, but the way he develops this stand turns the concept of deontology upside down.

Rawls accepts Frankena's conception of ethics as structured by the distinction and the relation between what is right and what is good. Teleology simply defines what is right to do in terms of what is good (Rawls 1971/99, 21), and deontological theories are defined as non-teleological, as theories that either do not specify the good independently from the right, or do not interpret the right as maximizing the good. Rawls prefers this logical conception of deontology as non-teleology to the view "that characterizes the rightness of institutions and acts independently from their consequences", i.e. Broad's first characterization of deontology and Weber's conception of the ethics of intention. Such a conception of ethics is to Rawls simply 'irrational, crazy' (1971/99, 26).

To Rawls, the concept of rationality is embodied in teleology; to be rational is simply to "strive for as high an absolute score as possible" (1971/99, 125).

With this identification of rationality with means-end rationality Rawls thus stays within the overall teleological conception of ethics exposed above,[16] and that strategy does not leave him much choice when utilitarianism and deontology as ethics of intention are ruled out. Staying within the classifications of Sidgwick et al. there is only one conceptual possibility, namely 'enlightened' egoism (Frankena 1963, 16), or self-regarding deontology, as Bentham would call it, and that is actually what Rawls ends up with. His concept of rationality thus in the end becomes equal to the means-end rationality of the inherently selfish *homo economicus* as construed by Weber. This should, however, not come as a surprise given Rawls' interest in game theory and contractual theories (cf. Rawls 1958); the weight put on rational self-interest was clearly visible from the very first conception of "justice as fairness" (Hall 1957, 663). Contracting parties always employ the rationality of game theory, i.e. the rationality of economic man, where each is supposed to maximize rationally his own long-term good.[17]

Apparently Rawls has forgotten that not every opposition to utilitarianism "by definition" is deontological, i.e. that egoism can be considered a teleological opposition to utilitarianism (Frankena 1963, 14). To Rawls, deontology is simply non-teleology, which is equal to non-utilitarianism. Therefore, deontology does not exclude rational egoism, and that makes it possible to let the alleged lack of concern for persons in utilitarianism – because of its impartiality – to be filled out by selfish partiality. A contract between two rational egoists is thus "by definition" for Rawls an expression of deontology.

Unfortunately, Rawls' understanding of his own practical philosophy as deontological has been widely accepted, and when deontology is understood as an expression of "agent-centered" restrictions on the strictly moral utilitarianism, then that position easily becomes equivalent to endorsing egoism. In sum, then, Rawls' political philosophy does not have much to contribute to ethics. Rawls' contract is based on a concept of man as totally selfish, whereas utilitarians at least accept man as inherently moral in some sense. Ethics simply presupposes that human beings do not want to be just selfish, but have sincere and serious doubts about what systematic egoist behaviour would imply for real human life. Economic man, however, is constructed as totally immoral – he does not even have a moral sense – and accepting the way Rawls opposes utilitarianism thus means as a moral-philosopher to leave the sphere of ethics as such.

In fact, Rawls could have chosen other strategies to oppose utilitarianism, but he fails to do so. He knows from Frankena that ethics is supposed to be rational, but he can only understand rationality in terms of rational choice theories (1971/99, 123-24), and that makes even a thoroughly logical consistent ethics of intention irrational, since it does not calculate the consequences. He can only understand consistency as Broad's concept of logical consistency, i.e. consistency in action, choosing the right means in view of the optimal realization of a given end. In contrast to Weber, Rawls cannot see that it is only from the limited perspective of means-end rationality that deontology and the ethics of intention are irrational, because Rawls has only this one concept of rationality.

It is precisely the concept of rationality as deductive rationality or, simply, reason, that Kant – and the neo-Kantian, Weber – understands to be central to ethics, and which Rawls ignores. It is precisely this idea of rationality that makes the Kantian distinction between acting in accordance with duty and acting out of duty meaningful; ethics is concerned with how to act out of duty, how to make such an act reasonable (Kant 1785/86, 20-22). Kant is not at all worried about the actual actions of people; he wants to justify their actions with reasons related to the law of reason. Kant wants to understand people as free, autonomous, self-legislative, subjugated only to the law of reason, the reason, which is our human nature.

In fact, the case of Rawls can be seen as tragic. Rawls explicitly wants to oppose utilitarianism in Sidgwick's version (Rawls 1971/99, 26), but in choosing to identify with deontology in Frankena's sense, he actually stays within Sidgwick's utilitarian scheme of thought, although transmitted through the more refined vocabulary of Broad and Frankena. Furthermore, he explicitly wants to identify with Kant (Rawls 1971/99, xviii), but as far as I can see, he simply does not understand the fundamentals of Kantian ethics.[18] Rawls describes Kant as giving priority to the right over the good (Rawls 1971/99, 28), and in the classification of Frankena this means that Kant is a deontologist; but, as mentioned above, Kant is only a deontologist when considered from within the perspective of Broad's refinement of Sidgwick's classification. Frankena simply misunderstands this point, claiming that Kant "purports to be" (Frankena 1963, 26) a deontologist, and this misunderstanding is apparently transmitted to Rawls. However, even without the misrepresentation of Frankena, Rawls would, with his very limited notion of rationality, have missed what Kant is talking about.[19]

*

Deontology was constructed by Bentham, but got its philosophical significance from Broad's classical distinction. Today, however, Broad's distinction is known primarily through Frankena, who codified it to be relevant only within normative ethics. With this in mind, one final thing should be noticed, i.e. the small shift in focus from Broad's first conception of the distinction to the second. In the discussion of the application of ought, Broad defines deontology in terms of the disregard for the consequences of an action. Teleology is not defined in terms of consequences, but in terms of the ends of an action. In the second version of the distinction, both deontology and teleology are defined in terms of consequences, the former through disregard and the latter through both the ends and the "tendency to produce certain consequences".

To Broad, this shift means very little, since he thinks of consequences only as "intended consequences" (*F.T.*, 210) as far as they can be "foreseen" (*F.T.*, 213); it is, however, of major significance. As long as teleology is defined in terms of ends, one can, as Rawls does, label an ethical theory like Aristotle's as teleological.[20] The shift of focus in teleology from ends to actions and their consequences, however, makes both the category of teleology more exclusive and the identification of teleology and utilitarianism much stronger. This shift pushes Aristotle over to the side of deontology, as in Frankena's classification. If such a strong identification is combined with an overall teleological – or, later, consequentialist – conception of ethics, there is hardly any sense left for deontology, either as an ethics of intention, or as any other kind of ethics.

Today this displacement is almost complete. On the one hand, the original teleology-deontology distinction is now normally understood as identical with consequentialism-deontology or even consequentialism-non-consequentialism. On the other hand, discussions about utilitarianism have been reformulated into discussions about consequentialism.[21] With the help of Frankena's classificatory skills, Broad's ideal-typical distinction has developed into a complete and non-arbitrary classification, which by definition – by law of the excluded middle – covers the whole field of normative ethics.

This is clearly a logical improvement, making the distinction simple and complete, just like Broad's own clarification of Sidgwick's classification was a step forward in this sense. But by making it logically stricter, Frankena actually emptied deontology of any positive content, while at the same time making it the only possibility for opposing utilitarianism. But having an exclusive and strict distinction between two types of ethical theories, where one of the aspects is impossible to take seriously, amounts to having no real distinction at all. And what is worse, the negative definition of deontology and Rawls' influential misunderstandings have made it possible for consequentialism to monopolize the idea of impartiality in ethics and to interpret the so-called agent relativity of deontology as partiality. This means that deontology is understood as egoism and thereby, "by definition", is inadmissible for most people as an ethical position.

From the very beginning deontology has been defined within a utilitarian scheme of thought. Deontology was constructed by Bentham, reconstructed by Broad in a completely different, but still utilitarian sense, first as an ideal limit and later as the marginal aspect of an exclusive distinction. Frankena generalized the logical definition, and this displacement was accepted by Rawls, who, however, was caught in the middle on the way from ideal limits to logical completeness. Whatever the reason, he turned things upside down, constructing the modern conception of deontology as virtually egoistic, a conception which is actually close to Bentham's original conception,[22] but is the opposite of Broad's and Frankena's. In a way, the circle is then closed. No matter which conception of deontology is chosen, accepting 'deontology' as a meaningful expression is submitting to the utilitarian scheme of thought. And if one finally asks why utilitarianism has had such an attraction within ethics, part of the answer is no doubt that it promises a conceptual development without having to bring troublesome concepts such as the self, intention and freedom into consideration (Ashby 1950, 772-73).

Literature

Apel, K.-O. (1993), "Das Anliegen des anglo-amerikanischen 'Kommunitarismus' in der Sicht der Diskursethik", in M. Brumlik and H. Brunkhorst (eds.), *Gemeinschaft und Gerechtigkeit* (Frankfurt a.M.: Fischer).

Aranguren, J.L.L. (1958), *Etica* in Aranguren, *Obras completas*, vol. 2 (Madrid: Trotta, 1994).

Aristotles (*Eth.Nic.*), *Nikomachische Ethik* (Berlin: Akademie Verlag, 1956) 1991.

Ashby, W. (1950), "Teleology and Deontology in Ethics", *Journal of Philosophy*, 47, 765-73.

Benn, P. (1998), *Ethics* (London: UCL Press).

Bentham, J. (*Deont.*, *Util.*), *Deontology together with A table of the springs of action and the article on Utilitarianism* in Bentham, *The collected works of...*, ed. by A. Goldworth (Oxford: Clarendon Press, 1983).

Bloom, A. (1975), "Justice: John Rawls Vs. The Tradition of Political Philosophy", *American Political Science Review*, 69, 648-62.

Broad, C.D. (1930), (*F.T.*), *Five Types of Ethical Theory* (London: Kegan Paul, Trench, Trubner & Co., 1944).

Broad, C.D. (1985), *Ethics* (Dordrecht: Martinus Nijhoff).

Brook, R. (1991), "Agency and Morality", *The Journal of Philosophy* 88, 190-212.
Campbell Garnett, A. (1941), "Deontology and Self-Realization", *Ethics*, 51, 419-38.
Campbell Garnett, A. (1956), "The Indicative Element in Deontological Words", *Ethics*, 67, 42-52.
Canto-Sperber, M. (ed.) (1996), *Dictionaire d'éthique et de philosophie morale* (Paris: P.U.F., 2001).
Carmichael, P.A. (1949), "The Logical Ground of Deontology", *The Journal of Philosophy*, 46, 29-41.
Davis, N.(A.) (1991), "Contemporary deontology", in: Singer 1991.
Darwall, S. (1986), "Agent-centered restrictions from the Inside Out", *Philosophical Studies* 50, 291-319.
Derrida, J. (1967), "Un hégelianisme sans réserve", *L'arc*, 32, 24-45.
Derrida, J. (1968), "La pharmacie de Platon" in Derrida, *La dissémination* (Paris: Seuil, 1972).
Edel, A. (1937), "Two Traditions in the Refutation of Egoism", *The Journal of Philosophy*, 34, 617-28.
Edel, A. (1973), "Right and Good", in P.P. Wiener (ed.), *Dictionary of the History of Ideas*, Vol. IV (New York: Charles Scribner's Sons).
Ellis, A. (1992), "Deontology, Incommensurability and the Arbitrary", *Philosophy and Phenomenological Research*, 52, 855-75.
Ferrater Mora, J. (1994), *Diccionario de filosofía* (Barcelona: Ariel).
Frankena, W.K. (1963), *Ethics* (Englewood Cliffs: Prentice-Hall).
Frankena, W.K. and J.T. Granrose (eds.) (1974), *Introductory Readings in Ethics* (Englewood Cliffs: Prentice-Hall).
Freeman, S. (1994), "Utilitarianism, Deontology, and the Priority of Right", *Philosophy and Public Affairs*, 23, 313-49.
Freeman, S. (2003), "Introduction" in Freeman (ed.), *The Cambridge Companion to Rawls* (Cambridge: Cambridge University Press).
Gauss, G.F. (2001a), "What is Deontology? Part One: Orthodox Views", *The Journal of Value Inquiry*, 35, 27-42.
Gauss, G.F. (2001b), "What is Deontology? Part Two: Reasons to Act", *The Journal of Value Inquiry*, 35, 179-93.
Goldworth, Amnon (1983), "Editoral Introduction" in Bentham, *Deont.*.
Habermas, J. (1991), *Erläuteringen zur Diskursethik* (Frankfurt a.M.: Suhrkamp).
Halévy, E., (1901-04), *The Growth of Philosophic Radicalism* (Boston: Beacon Press, 1955).
Hall, E.W (1957), "II. Justice as Fairness: A Modernized Version of the Social Contract", *The Journal of Philosophy*, 54, 662-70.
Kant, I. (1785/86), *Grundlagen zur Metaphysik der Sitten* in Kant, *Schriften zur Ethik und Religionsphilosophie (Werke in Sechs Bänden, Band IV)*, ed. by W. Wieschedel (1956) (Darmstadt: Wissenschaftliche Buchgesellschaft, 1998).
Kutschera, F.v. (1982), *Grundlagen der Ethik* (Berlin & New York: Walter de Gruyter).
Kymlicka, W. (1988), "Rawls on Teleology and Deontology", *Philosophy and Public Affairs*, 17, 173-90.
Lalande, A. (1991), *Vocabulaire technique et critique de la philosophie*, 18^e ed. (Paris: Presses Universitaires de France).
Muirhead, J.H. (1940), "The New Deontology", *Ethics*, 50, 441-49.
Nowell-Smith, P.H. (1954), *Ethics* "Harmondsworth: Penguin".
Nagel, T. (1986), *The View from Nowhere* (New York: Oxford University Press).

Postema, G.J. (2006), "Bentham's Utilitarianism" in H.R. West (ed.), *The Blackwell Guide to Mill's Utilitarianism* (Oxford: Blackwell).
Rawls, J. (1958), "Justice as Fairness" in Rawls, *Collected Papers* (Cambridge, Mass.: Harvard University Press, 1999).
Rawls, J. (1971/99), *A Theory of Justice* (Cambridge, Mass.: Harvard University Press).
Ritter, J. (ed.) (1972), *Historiches Wörterbuch der Philosophie, Band 2 D-F* (Darmstadt: Wissenschaftlische Buchgesellschaft).
Ryan, A. (1987), "Introduction" in Ryan (ed.), *John Stuart Mill and Jeremy Bentham. Utilitarianism and Other Essays* (Harmondsworth: Penguin).
Salzman, T.A. (1995), *Deontology and Teleology* (Leuven University Press).
Scheffler, S. (1984), "Agent-Centered Restrictions, Rationality, and the Virtues", *Mind*, 94, 409-19.
Schneewind, J.B. (1977), *Sidgwick's Ethics and Victorian Moral Philosophy* (Oxford: Oxford University Press).
Schneewind, J.B. (1991), 'Modern moral philosophy', in: Singer 1991.
Singer, P. (ed.) (1991), *A Companion to Ethics* (Oxford: Blackwell).
Stegmüller, W. (1989), *Hauptströmungen der Gegenwartsphilosophie, Bd. IV* (Stuttgart: Alfred Kröner).
Sørensen, A. (2003), *Forskning, etik, konsekvens* (København: Politisk Revy).
Weber, M. (1919), "Politik als Beruf" in Weber, *Gesammelte Politische Schriften* (Tübingen: J.C.B. Mohr, 1988).
Weber, M. (1922), "Die 'Objektivität' sozialwissenschaftlischer und sozialpolitischer Erkenntnis" in Weber, *Gesammelte Aufsätze zur Wissenschaftslehre* (Tübingen: J.C.B. Mohr, 1988).
Weber, M. (1921-22), *Wirtschaft und Gesellschaft* (Tübingen: J.C.B. Mohr, 1990).

Notes

1. This article has in various versions passed through many hands and been presented in many places. I would therefore like to thank the following for valuable criticism, suggestions, and comments on earlier versions: Anders Bordum, Asmund Born, Bent Meier Sørensen, Brian Barry, Christine Korsgaard, Helen Korsgaard, Jacob Vestergaard, Roberto Mordacci, Robin May Schott, Sergio Cremaschi, Steen Valentin and Thomas Basbøll.
2. Normally, Bentham's utilitarian ethics is extracted from his *An Introduction to the Principles of Morals and Legislation* (cf. e.g. Ryan 1987, 9), and in spite of the fact that *Deontology* is Bentham's only attempt to develop systematically the moral philosophy implied by utilitarianism, one rarely sees any references to it in ethical debates about utilitarianism. An exception is Edel, whose systematic conception of utilitarianism is informed by *Deontology* (1937, 620).
3. In a recent anthology on Mill's *Utilitarianism*, Bentham's construction of the term 'deontology' is noticed (Postema 2006, 28), but without any reflections about the possible terminological and conceptual consequences.
4. It is from this perspective that Kymlicka can criticize Rawls for confusing things, precisely because Rawls thinks of teleology as including perfectionism (Kymlicka 1988, 185-88).
5. In fact, I would like to claim that the history of Anglophone ethics in the twentieth century can be reconstructed as an on-going refinement and development of distinctions forced upon ethics by the insistent pressure of the utilitarians with their amoral preconception of ethics. Since this point is too general to be argued convincingly within the limits of an article, I will

constrain myself to analyse this – I think – crucial and very clear case as an illustration of the more general story.
6. This bi-partition is apparently the result of an editorial decision. Whether this also was Bentham's own division is not altogether clear in Goldworth's commentary (Goldworth 1983, xixff., xxixff.), but it seems to be in accordance with Bentham's general line of thought.
7. Although, admittedly, we must then assume that Bentham forgot to qualify the definition of deontology as concerned with private morality as a definition of *private* deontology.
8. Broad's refinement of Sidgwick's classification makes it possible to think of ethics as divided into two branches, one concerned only with epistemology and questions of meaning, i.e. meta-ethics, and one pretending not to be concerned with these matters at all, normative ethics, thought to be totally independent from meta-ethics. This is another instance of the more general phenomenon in Anglophone ethics mentioned above, namely that utilitarianism plays the decisive role in the continuous development of the increasingly refined ethical distinctions. It would, however, require much more research and analysis to substantiate my claim, and in this context the matter is further obscured by the fact that Broad describes his own distinction as ontological (Broad 1930, 213).
9. The conception of deontology as defined positively in relation to the mode of the action in question, and the intrinsic rightness of this mode, can also be found in modern continental European interpretation treatments of ethics (Kutschera 1982, 2; Stegmüller 1989, 231). In Gaus' analysis of the Anglo-American discussions, however, this conception is not given much attention (cf. Gaus 2001a, 36 and 2001b, 183).
10. Salzman insists that the distinction is altogether meta-ethical (Salzman 1995, 4), but this mistake must rest on his identification of the analytical approach to ethics with meta-ethics as such (1995, 32).
11. Even today, Frankena can be considered the suitable starting point for a comprehensive analysis of deontology (Gaus 2001a, 27), bypassing thereby both Bentham and Broad.
12. It should be noted that this focus, already implicit in Bentham's utilitarianism, is the exact opposite of the traditional, pre-modern ethical focus (cf. e.g. Aranguren 1958, 182).
13. This quote is the only one by Aristotle in Ross' analysis of the right and the good (cf. e.g. Ross 1930, 42), and one might suspect that Frankena simply has copied it from Ross.
14. Instead, in the posthumously published manuscripts Broad uses the term 'deontic' to characterize all sentences employing words like 'duty', 'obligation' and the like (Broad 1985, 225). In this sense, 'deontic' thus comes close to the general conception of deontology as a science of duties, and such a conception makes it possible for Broad to compare anew Kant with Ross and Sidgwick. However, since he considers the categorical imperative 'vague' (Broad 1985, 219), the only two possibilities are "the irreducible pluralism of Ross" and the utilitarian "theory of a single ultimate self-evident obligation", which "have strong claims to be considered self-evident" (Broad 1985, 242), and which do not leave deontology many chances within ethics.
15. Gaus fails to find one positive definition common to the various current uses of 'deontology'. The only common denominator is negative, namely the opposition to consequentialism (Gaus 2001b, 190).
16. In fact, the teleological conception of rationality is such a commonplace in Anglophone discussions of these matters that it often passes unnoticed, as for instance in Freeman's defence of Rawls against the critique of Kymlicka (Freemann 1994, 313).
17. Freeman denies that Rawls' contracting parties in the original position are egoists (Freeman 2003, 13), since they allegedly have a capacity for justice. Still, he describes them as "con-

cerned only with promoting their own interests" (2003, 14), which is precisely what egoism is about.
18. Allan Bloom points to the same differences in the understanding of rationality between Rawls and Kant, and argues convincingly that the thought of Rawls "has nothing to do with that of Kant" (Bloom 1975, 657).
19. The contrast between the Hobbesian concepts of rationality common in Anglo-American practical philosophy and Kant's concept of reason is underlined strongly by Apel (Apel 1993, 152-54).
20. Aristotle takes as his point of departure what man strives toward, *i.e.* an end, and later – after various analyses of the dynamic character of moral and intellectual virtues – defines this end as the good life, where happiness consists in actions in conformity with virtues (cf. *Eth.Nic.*, 1176). Broad, however, does not categorize the ethics of Aristotle as teleological; in fact, Aristotle is not mentioned in *Five Types* at all.
21. With almost all the moral weight put on the consequences as such, the intended end is now treated as only of minor moral importance, and this creates new ethical problems, like those of acts and omissions and the so-called double-effect (cf. Benn 1998, 74, 78).
22. The biographer of Bentham, Elie Halévy, simply concludes that to Bentham "egoism [was] installed at the very basis of morality" (Halévy 1901-04, 477).

BODY AND MOTION IN EARLY MODERN PHILOSOPHY OF NATURE: NEWTON AGAINST DESCARTES

SUNE FRØLUND

Department of Philosophy of Education
School of Education, University of Aarhus

ABSTRACT. The article addresses the connection of theory of knowledge with physics in Descartes and Newton. The establishment of a geometric concept of motion in Descartes' mechanistic physics required an epistemic subject with strong constructional powers. Descartes found this in the disembodied, supernatural I. Newton's reintroduction of forces in his kinematics, however, made him accuse Descartes' interpretation of motion for being non-realistic and contradictory. It also made him attack the mind-body-dualism as the false basis for Cartesian physics. In Newton's physics only an embodied soul could acquire knowledge of the real motion, force and action of (other) natural bodies. The article presents central parts of this debate.

1. Nature – activity or structure?

The development of early modern natural science implied a replacement of the older substance metaphysics with a structuralist view of nature. For pre-modern natural philosophy the basic ontological unit was the individual thing, whereas the new perspective focused on the external relations between things. The shift of perspective was implemented through polemics against the idea that natural things are 'substances', i.e. agents having an internal 'nature', an 'essence' or a 'form' that determines their activities or movements. After all, agency was eliminated from substances – things could be dissolved into particles of specific quantities that were linked in structures made up of geometrical or mathematical relationships (Boudri 2002, 28ff.).

The abstraction from autonomous thing to relational structure required a much stronger emphasis on the epistemic activity of the subject. This, again, required an emancipation of the knowing subject from its earthly, bodily or natural restraint. A mind-body dualism was introduced in order to set free the constructional powers of the subject. The 'Copernican Turn' in astronomy can be considered the paradigm for this liberation of the subject to adopt an external viewpoint or even a view from nowhere.

The importance of this perspectivism for the development of science cannot be overestimated. Yet the separation of the subject from the body also created epistemological problems that challenged realism in scientific knowledge and gave rise to major disputes between philosophers of nature and scientists.

The substance metaphysics of the Aristotelian tradition was sustained by the bodily experiences of the subject. In this tradition the rational soul was embodied, and the inner experience of *being* a body, even of being a *living* body, was the primary experience of any physical body and its activities in general. The natural science of this tradition was, consequently, built upon these bodily experiences. This was the case with such concepts from Aristotelian physics as substance, cause and motion, as well as with the Aristotelian concept of nature itself (Spaemann 1987, 20ff.).[1] But when monistic ontology was abandoned with the formation of early modern mechanics, the older concepts were either eliminated or – more commonly – reinterpreted to better fit a dualistic ontology. This was in particular the case with dynamical concepts like movement, force, power, cause, impulse, striving, endeavour, etc. As could be expected, the mixture of old and new interpretations gave rise to a large number of incoherent theories and many disputes, especially in the seventeenth and the eighteenth centuries.

In this article I shall present one of the lesser known disputes on the connection of mechanics with bodily experience. We know of the pivotal role played by the separation of mind from body in the epistemology and physics of René Descartes (1596-1650), because Descartes published the philosophical background for his natural science. In contrast, little is known of Isaac Newton's (1642-1727) philosophy of nature, since so little of it was published by the author. This, however, should not make us believe that Newton was indifferent to philosophical matters or to Cartesian philosophy in particular. In fact, the study of Descartes' physics and philosophy was an important step for Newton in developing his own physics. This article will focus on Newton's rejection of Cartesian dualism and on his arguments for the importance of embodied knowledge for the true understanding of nature. I shall start by outlining the traditional picture of Newton.

2. Newton vs. Newtonianism

Thanks to British and French Enlightenment philosophers of the eighteenth century, Newton was stylized as the rupture of natural science with pre-modern natural philosophy. Newton was considered an epitome of austere rationality and a cult of Newtonianism was erected (Dobbs and Jacob 1995). Newton was pictured as having developed his mechanics and optics independent of all ontological concerns. He had allegedly rebuffed the search for the 'true causes' and 'true purposes' of nature, and was also said to take no interest in the arcane search for the specific natures of force, matter, movement, space and time. Notions like these were applied only for pragmatic reasons and had, it was claimed, no bearing on natural philosophy. In particular the idea of gravitation was introduced for pure methodological reasons, or was interpreted as a sheer empirical concept. Newton was, in short, pictured as a fully fledged positivist, and his famous words "hypotheses non fingo" was praised as his scientific credo.[2]

The exorcism of natural philosophy and metaphysics from natural science was so effective that only a hundred years after Newton's *Philosophiae Naturalis Principia Mathematica* (1687) natural science was considered to be an autonomous discipline that did not need the services of philosophy. When Immanuel Kant published his *Metaphysische Anfangsgründe der Naturwissenschaft* (1786), he accepted that philosophy (metaphysics) was no longer an integral part of science.[3]

The last fifty years of Newton scholarship has radically corrected the picture of Newton and disclosed the incompatibility of Newton and Newtonianism. The decisive change took place in 1936 when a large body of manuscripts – many of which were judged unsuitable for publication by the trustee of Newton's estate – was sold by auction. Surprisingly, only a minority of the manuscripts treated mathematical or physical subjects, and of these only a few treated genuine mechanics or optics. The vast majority of the manuscripts were discourses on theology, revelation, chronology, history, patristics (and studies of other 'wise ancients') and on alchemy. Newton's interest in theological and chronological matters had indeed been known by his contemporaries. This occupation was, however, played down as studies "with which he used to amuse himself after the fatigue of his severer studies" (Voltaire 1733, Letter XV). Less mentioned or known were Newton's alchemic studies and practice, which were far more unpardonable. Not until the last ten to fifteen years has alchemy been generally recognized as an integral part of Newton's multi-faceted search for the 'unity of Truth'. It has even been argued that the influence of alchemy was responsible for Newton's reintroduction of forces of attraction and, consequently, for being the basis for the success of his mechanics (Dobbs 1991, 6ff.).[4]

3. *On gravitation* – a philosophical Newton text

Here I shall turn to the genuinely philosophical side of Newton. One of the texts that surfaced in 1936 revealed the philosopher Newton in a vehement debate with Descartes on the ontology and epistemology of movement, space and force. This is highly interesting, as Newton surprisingly only mentioned Descartes four times in his *Principia*, despite there being a good chance that Descartes' *Principia Philosophiae* (1644) acted as a model when Newton worked out his own *Principia*. Firstly, Descartes' book was the most comprehensive work on natural philosophy and science since Aristotle, and, secondly, the two works exhibited a large number of similarities in their titles, choice of topics, composition, definitions of concepts and wording of laws.[5]

The text referred to bears no title but is commonly named after its inceptive words: *De gravitatione et aequipondio fluidorum et solidorum, On the Gravitation and Equilibrium of Fluids and Solids*. In the following I shall call it *On gravitation* (Newton 1962).[6] To support the presumption that *On gravitation* grants us more of the philosophical, i.e. epistemological considerations, that Newton omitted in the final edition of *Principia* and that he was in general so chary of uttering in public, we will have to dwell a little on the question of the dating of the text.

There is no dispute that the text dates from Newton's pre-*Principia* period; the question is how tightly it can be linked to the composition of *Principia*. The first editors of *On gravitation* judged it to be a juvenile piece of work from the mid-1660s, when Newton's reading of Descartes was fresh and he was still tempted to discuss philosophy (Hall and Hall 1962, 90). A number of other estimates have moved the text to a later date, but no later than the mid-1670s. It has, however, never escaped the attention of scholars that *On gravitation* has striking thematic, structural and conceptual parallels to *Principia* (Koyré 1965, 82; Dobbs 1991, 139ff.).

In the following I shall assume that *On gravitation* should be assigned to the years just before the writing of the *Principia*, i.e. in mid-1680s. A few considerations can support this assumption. Firstly, the methodological considerations in *On gravitation* anticipate the *Principia*. *On gravitation* will present its mathematical demonstrations in "lemmas, propositions and corollaries" but will also make "clear many of the phenomena of natural philosophy" using a "freer method of discussion, disposed in scholia" (Newton 1992, 121). This is paralleled in the *Principia*'s main text and in the 'freer' scholias scattered all over the entire work, respectively. Secondly, the subjects of *On gravitation* – gravitation and equilibrium in liquids and in massive bodies in liquids – correspond to the themes of Book 1 and Book 2 of the *Principia*. And, thirdly, the concept of 'innate force', i.e. inertia, which plays a pivotal role in the *Principia,* is introduced for the first time in *On gravitation.* The most convincing arguments for the dating of *On gravitation* to the first half of the 1680s, however, is in my view provided by Dobbs' careful studies of Newton's changing positions on gravity throughout his entire scientific development (Dobbs 1991, 130-46).

Roughly speaking, Newton's position on the cause of gravity ran through three stages. As a young man he adopted Descartes' vortex and ether theory as the explanation of centripetal forces or attraction between bodies. According to this theory, gravitational effects are due to the mechanical impact of particles of an imperceptible ether.

A growing awareness that celestial movements do not show retardation, as was expected if space was filled with ether, and a series of pendulum experiments, which failed to detect any ether, convinced Newton of the fallacy of Descartes' explanation of gravity. Based on evidence from other texts than *On gravitation* this change can be dated to the year 1684. Three years later, in *Principia,* the new stance was reflected in the doctrine of empty space, in the persistent attacks on vortices, and in the introduction of 'attraction' as the force behind gravity.[7]

At the turn of the century Newton's continued search for the cause of gravity had made him reintroduce an ether. This time, however, it was not a plenistic, but an immaterial ether, a 'subtle spirit' that did not work as a 'mechanical cause'. This new stance was expressed in the famous "General Scholium", added in the second edition of the *Principia* (from 1713), and in the "Queries" of Newton's *Opticks* (Newton 1999, 939ff.).[8]

Dobbs' reconstruction of this development supports her suggestion that *On gravitation* is *the* text in which Newton's general showdown with Descartes takes place. It makes her date the text to 1684 (Dobbs 1991, 132).[9]

4. Newton's attack on Descartes' relativism

The text embarks on definitions of place, body, rest and motion, and then breaks off for a 26-page note, before continuing for eigth more pages with fifteen other definitions, a number of axioms, propositions, demonstrations, corrolaries, etc., and then suddenly ends. It is the long, digressive note that attracts our primary interest.

Newton opens the note by expressing his opposition to two Cartesian doctrines: that matter equals extension and that all movements of a body are relative. According to Newton's definitions, place (*locus*) is a part of space, and body is that which "fills place". Consequently space and body are distinct. This makes it possible for Newton to define the motion of bodies relative to parts of space, which should be considered at rest in an absolute sense, rather than relative to other bodies, as Descartes does. To confirm that his opposition to Descartes is by no means "gratuitous", as he puts it, Newton launches a general attack on Descartes' mechanics to "dispose of his [Descartes'] fictions" (Newton 1962, 123). Newton refers to a number of central sections from part II and III of Descartes' *Principia Philosophiae* (*PPh*), and to these I shall now devote some attention.

The identification of body and extension leaves Descartes with no other option for locating a body than through its relations to other bodies. There is no fixed location for anything except "in our thoughts", he says (*PPh*, II, 13).[10] A consequence of this is that "the same thing can at the same time be said to change position and not change position, and be said to move and not move" (II, 24). Descartes is aware that this is against the 'vulgar' parlance (*ex vulgi uso*), which interprets movement as an 'action' (*actio*) displaying a 'force' and considers rest to be the cessation of action. He contrasts the common assumption with the 'philosophical' definition of movement, which is "according to the truth" (*ex rei veritate*), and which runs as follows: "the translation of a part of matter, or of a body, from the neighbourhood of what it immediately touches, and that is considered at rest, to the neighbourhood of some others" (II, 24, 25). From this geometric definition of movement it follows that movement and rest are nothing but "two modes" (*duo diversi modi,* II, 27) of a body. The mode that is perceived depends on the body's different external relations. Specifically it depends on which relata "we consider to be at rest" (II, 29). Motion is not an internal property of a body, but depends on the observer's perspective and choice of relata.

A body can be a part of various other bodies and participate in these bodies' movements. But, as it is not in our power to know all of these movements, "it is sufficient that we consider the movement for each body that is unique, and of which we can have certain knowledge" (*PPh*, II, 31). Descartes here refers to his definition of movement, in which the relata should be the immediately touched, local bodies. From this he draws the surprising consequence that neither the Earth nor the other planets move in the true sense of the term. The planets are not transferred away from the contiguous parts of the sky, which Descartes considers to be fluent matter, i.e. an ether.[11] The ether, however, is rotating in several vortices, and the vortices conduct the Earth and the other planets with it, but still "the Earth is at rest in its heaven which nevertheless carries it along" (III, 26). Descartes likewise rejects the idea that the Earth moves in relation to the fixed stars. Firstly, the fixed stars are not contiguous with the Earth and cannot therefore be used to determine motion. Secondly, the stars can only be said to be immovable if one believes the world is limited, but this would be against good reason, Descartes explains (III, 29). For without doubt there are more bodies behind the fixed stars, in relation to which they themselves move, and in relation to which the Earth is at rest (III, 29, 30).

Turning our attention back to *On gravitation,* it is easy enough to imagine Newton's anger at Descartes' contradistinction between the 'vulgar' account of space and movement and the 'true' or 'philosophical' account. It is clear that Newton identifies himself with the former. And he maintains that Descartes tacitly presupposes the vulgar account that he appears to reject, i.e. contradicts himself. Newton now presents a series of arguments to substantiate this allegation.

First of all, Newton points out that Descartes ascribes to the Earth a "tendency to recede", i.e. an inertial tendency to move in a straight line in its curved motion around the sun. But this is only possible if the Earth actually moves in the 'vulgar' sense. Secondly, Newton accuses Descartes of turning movements into mental fictions, when he defines movement relative to a contiguous body that "*we consider* to be in rest" (as Descartes says in *PPh* II, 25, my italics). Thirdly, Descartes is inconsistent when he also claims that the reciprocal relation between a moving body and the contiguous body is valid (*PPh* II, 30), since this would imply that we consider both bodies to be moving and at rest at the same time. Fourthly, Descartes' definition of movement relative to the contiguous matter renders the interior parts of a body to be at rest even if Descartes accepts that the body's surface moves (which is absurd). In the fifth place, Descartes cannot consistently claim that a body only has one single motion but at the same time participates in innumerable other motions as well. In Newton's view this is only possible if one accepts that bodies have one true, 'absolute' motion, and "that the rest of its changes of relation of position with respect to other bodies are so many external designations" (Newton 1962, 127). Newton adds that the movement of the Earth that causes it to "endeavour to recede from the Sun is to be declared the Earth's natural and absolute motion. Its translations relative to external bodies [i.e. the other planets] are but external designations" (Newton 1962, 127).

Newton extends his criticism to Descartes' account of comets and vortices. Descartes had explained the increased speed of comets approaching the sun as the result of their entrance into the faster gyration of vortices closer to the sun. But this is only a valid explanation if the vortices themselves have a tangential 'striving' – which Descartes indeed concedes (*PPh,* III, 119, 140) – but this the vortices can *not* have, as Newton points out, if they are to serve as the motionless contiguous matter to the alleged non-movement of planets. And how can vortices be said to move circularly on account of the translation of matter near their circumference, if the matter of the surrounding vortices is not at rest (Newton 1962, 129)? In sum, Newton concludes, the philosopher – Descartes – should acknowledge "motion in the vulgar sense … rather than the philosophical" (Newton 1962, 125).

Newton now moves on to discuss Descartes' abandonment of the notions of action and force. In Newton's eyes these concepts are indispensable, if we are to explain the generation or acceleration of movements. Imagine, Newton writes, that God suddenly stopped the vortex from spinning, but did not force the Earth to stop. In this situation Descartes would be compelled to say that the Earth suddenly had started to move, since its relation to the ethereal matter of the vortex was altered. But who, Newton appeals to the 'vulgar' opinion, would ascribe a rising motion to the very body that had *no* force imposed upon it (Newton 1962, 128)? This rhetorical question points to counter-intuitive consequences of a fully externalistic account of movements like Descartes'.

The final argument against the Cartesian account is a rather sophisticated one. Newton demonstrates that Descartes' definition of movement in general renders it impossible to ascribe a *definite* speed or trajectory to a moving body. Following Descartes' definition, the position of a moving body can only be assigned by the actual position of the surrounding bodies. But, as the positions of these bodies cannot be determined or fixed *after* the moving body has moved away, it is simply meaningless to talk of any past position of a moving body.

And this, again, means that when the body has moved away "the place does not exist in nature any longer (*non amplius in rerum natura existit*)" (Newton 1962, 130). But, if it is not possible to determine a sequence of positions over time, it makes no sense to talk about a moving body's trajectory or velocity. It simply "cannot be said whence the body moved" (Newton 1962, 129).

Newton's concluding verdict on Descartes' kinematics is definitive: "Cartesian motion is not motion, for it has no velocity, no definition, and there is no space or distance traversed by it" (Newton 1962, 131).

5. Consequences of disembodied knowledge

One can wonder why it was so relatively easy for Newton to expose flaws and contradictions in Descartes' mechanics. Part of the explanation lies in the motivation and structure of the *Principia Philosophiae*. The ambition of this work was to compile the total outcome of Descartes' previous endeavours in physics and philosophy into a single textbook. The physics was already worked out in *Le Monde* (*The World*), which Descartes started to write in 1629. In this book he derived the heliocentric system from three laws of motion and added a theory of light. It was planned as the first part of a tripartite work that was to include a volume on the 'rational soul', providing the philosophical or metaphysical basis for Descartes' mechanistic cosmology. But the last volume was never written, and Descartes decided to abandon the publication of *Le Monde* because of the 1633 condemnation of Galileo's Copernican physics by the Roman Inquisition.

The philosophical foundation for Descartes' physics was eventually developed in the *Meditationes* of 1641. In this book an epistemology driven by scepticism was used to eliminate the world of common sense 'prejudices' and the world of Aristotelian natural philosophy. Two principles survived Descartes' methodical doubt: that genuine knowledge was based on "clear and distinct ideas", and that the subject of knowledge, the soul, was separated from the bodily nature. The first principle favoured a mathematical grasp of nature, the second favoured a mechanical, de-animated interpretation of changes in nature.

In the first part of *Principia*'s all-comprising system of natural philosophy, this epistemology was repeated. In the subsequent reconstruction of the natural world throughout the rest of the book, the notion of "clear and distinct ideas" drove Descartes to reformulate the physical theory he developed in *Le Monde*'s relatively 'dynamical' context using a new, more stringent, more economical vocabulary, which had recourse only to geometrically definable notions. Whereas dynamics can be defined as the theory of accelerating and decelerating forces and the movements they produce, kinematics describes movements in purely geometric terms. In this way kinematics avoids the difficulties of measuring forces, actions and causes, and focuses on the more operational measurements of position and time in a system of coordinates (Gaukroger 2002, 113).[12] When Descartes rephrased his mechanics in *Principia Philosophiae,* he would accordingly omit terms like 'action', 'force' and 'striving (*conatus*)' from his vocabulary, even if these terms lurked beneath the surface and challenged the consistency of his theory of motion.

The second principle, the psycho-physical dualism – itself supposedly given as a clear and distinct idea – was designed to prevent the risk of such inconsistency by giving ontological support to a geometrical-kinematical physics. Such dualism was a perfect tool to purify nature from 'obscure' notions derived from Aristotelian-Scholastic vocabulary, some of which were in alliance with common sense. What offended Descartes in notions such as 'form' or 'essence' was that they were purporting to be 'internal souls' (Perler 1999, 81) guiding matter and thus pretending to give epistemic access to 'inwardness' in the realm of nature. 'Occult' (hylozoist or anthropomorphist) pretensions like this were anathema to the externalist view of nature under construction.

The notions of force, action, cause and striving were indeed considered to be such obsolete concepts. Descartes considered their origin to be the close contact between the spiritual and corporeal substances from infancy, when "our mind was so closely tied to the body that it had no leisure for anything except for the impressions it caused" (*PPh,* I, 71). This contact gave us the false idea that the 'internal consciousness' we have of our ability to move our bodies through our will could be expanded to all cases of natural causation (II, 26). Descartes rejected the common experience of our embodied mind and the idea that we can have bodily knowledge, i.e. that we can have insider knowledge of (some) bodies. His alternative was that our identity only rests with our rational consciousness, ideally with that part of consciousness that processes quantity. Realizing this, we should now be able to decline the 'childish' idea that change and movement are activities demanding causing forces (I, 65).[13]

As a result of this change, the whole idea of motion departed from the Aristotelian conception. The change was, however, seldom pursued with genuine arguments or with demonstration of the defects of the older conception. Aristotle's fourfold movement was reduced to local movement, and all other changes – growth, generation, annihilation and change of quality – were reduced to local motions of particles (Gaukroger 2002, 180ff.). Descartes' only argument for this reduction in *Principia* was that he could not 'think' of any other kind of movement than local motion (*PPh*, II, 24). Growth and organic nutrition were explained resolutely in mechanical terms from size, shape and initial positions of materials in relation to organs (Gaukroger 2002, 190ff.). Generation and annihilation were in reality nothing but different combinations of imperishable material particles, and qualities were relegated to the unreliable senses of the embodied subject. The same fate befell Aristotle's general definition of motion. In *Le Monde* Descartes had quoted it, and simply declared it 'obscure', but in *Principia* he did not even mention it.[14] According to the Aristotelian definition, motion is "the actuality of what is potentially F, insofar as it is potentially F" (Aristotle, *Physics* 201b5). Again we can make out Descartes' problem with this definition: potentiality only makes sense when the bodily experiences of the agent are acknowledged. Being in a state of potentiality is *quasi* being in a state of anticipating future actualization, because we can only apprehend potentiality from what it has potentiality *to*, i.e. as a not-yet stage of its actualization.[15] Without recognizing the embodied consciousness of the agent during a time span before and after actualization, a definition like Aristotle's is senseless. But this consciousness is exactly what Descartes ignores. There is no epistemic access to agents or living bodies in his philosophy. He can thus construct a materialistic nature, in which any object always is what it fully and actually is. An entity in a state of potentiality has no reality for Descartes (Perler 1999, 78). And consequently the notion of causation is emptied of meaning or reduced to being simply what was temporally there *before*, or to what can be reconstructed as the necessary conditions for the present state.[16] Nothing is physically or bodily caused in Descartes' nature, and one can wonder if anything really *happens* there.

This is virtually what Newton's last argument – mentioned above – against Cartesian motion pinpointed. The absence of potentiality was closely connected to the discontinuity of Descartes' concept of time. In his view all the 'parts of time' are independent of each other (*PPh*, I, 21), hence there is no temporal unity and continuity from before till now and later. The world is only upheld thanks to God's constant recreation (II, 36).[17] Accordingly, a local position only exists in reality in the very moment the object is present at the position, not before or after it has moved away. Hence – as Newton pointed out – it makes no sense to talk of the speed or the trajectory of moving bodies, i.e. it makes no sense to talk of *real* motion at all.

The abandonment of force, potency and causes was not only a change in physics but it promoted a seminal change in the very conception of what it is to *know* something. When we make comparison with Aristotle's words from the *Physics*, this change is evident: "We think we know a thing when we know its primary causes and primary origin (*archai*)" (Aristotle, *Physics* 184a14). From Descartes onwards, the emphasis was on measurable, quantifiable effects, not on less evident causes or obscure forces leading to the effect. This is seen in the polemics against causes and forces in Locke, Hume and Voltaire, as well as in the physics of d'Alembert or – in the nineteenth century – of Mach, Kirchhoff, Hertz or Pearson (Frølund 2005, 92-111). Why things move was considered unimportant for the question of how things move.

6. Newton's alternative

Newton's cure for Descartes' non-realistic kinematics is to 'overthrow' (*eversio*) what he considers the basis of Cartesianism, namely the distinction between the thinking and the extended substances (Newton 1962, 99, 131). This he does 1) by depriving extension of the status of a substance, and turning it into a certain "disposition (*affectio*) of all being", deriving from an all-pervading "emanative effect of God" (Newton 1962, 132), 2) by giving thoughts and bodies united status as substantial entities, and 3) by defining substances as entities "that can act upon things" (like all philosophers 'tacitly' do, Newton 1962, 99, 132).

The immediate benefit of this ontology is a non-relativistic concept of motion.

Being the effect of God's eternal existence, extension is omnipresent, immutable and passive, and accordingly it can function as absolute space and absolute time. Newton can subsequently reinstall the 'vulgar' conception of motion as a real activity in nature. According to their different ontological status, however, space, time, and entities present different epistemological problems. The features of space and time are the necessary consequence of God's existence, hence a kind of *a priori* or 'abstract' reasoning is the proper procedure to analyze these two sides of extension. We all have a clear idea of extension when we abstract from the properties of bodies, Newton assures us. On the basis of these abstracted ideas we can tell that space and time may be unlimited, homogeneous, independent of any entity but include them all. No created entity ('substance') is outside time or space, even "created souls are somewhere" (Newton 1962, 136). Furthermore, space is three-dimensional and includes *a priori* all possible geometric forms. Doing geometry is discovering pre-existing forms and making them visible (Newton 1962, 133). Both space and time yield a structure upon which places and parts of space get their individual position and character, and upon which moments and time spans get their succession and irreversible order (Newton 1962, 136). And thanks to the continuity of time, past (and future) moments are preserved (or anticipated), so that it makes sense to talk about past (and future) stages of a movement as constituting the present reality of the movement.

The method of reasoning which Newton displays concerning extension is predominantly rationalistic and Cartesian. His view is inspired by a theory developed by the Platonic Cambridge philosopher Henry More (1614-1787) and presented as an alternative to Descartes' materialistic interpretation of nature. Even though More and Newton deviate from Descartes in detail, both reason about space and time on the basis of clear and distinct ideas and claim the outcome of this reasoning to be of logical necessity. The difference between the natural philosophies of Descartes and Newton is striking, however, when it comes to the epistemology of moving bodies. Here *a priori* reasoning is of no use. Interestingly, Newton rehabilitates the old tradition for thinking in analogy. He suggests that we transfer our own bodily experience to bodies in general.

Like most of his contemporaries, Newton believes the original creation of bodies and movements to be the result of God's will and free decision. This introduces a certain contingency or indeterminacy into the movements of bodies and, consequently, makes it comparatively more insecure to settle the nature of bodily activity. In this case our only chance epistemically is to start with "our innermost consciousness (*nobis intime conscijs*)" (Newton 1962, 107, 141) that we can move our bodies at will and "that all men enjoy the same power of similarly moving their bodies by thought alone" (Newton 1962, 138). From this experience we know that thoughts are agents in the corporeal world, i.e. that they are substances just like the bodies, which – conversely – have the force to "excite various perceptions of the senses and the fancy" (Newton 1962, 140). Furthermore, the experience of our own body informs us that "bodies may think, and a thinking being extend" (Newton 1962, 143), i.e. that the union of thought and body is a reality in some natural entities. And from this experience we are entitled to infer the nature and activities of other bodies.

An inference by analogy is a weak type of inference, and Newton readily admits that it gives no exact knowledge. It is further weakened because Newton wants the analogy to be partially indirect. He wants the analogy to pass through conjectures to the way God creates bodies and how He makes parts of space impervious to other bodies, so that they can act upon these other bodies. In this respect our faculties are limited. We cannot assume complete similarity between our own body and other bodies. In fact, we cannot even arbitrarily move other bodies, but only move our own body, and thereby indirectly move other bodies, thanks to our own body's impenetrability. Nor can we move bodies in any way we want, Newton adds, but only in accord with certain laws that God has imposed on us (Newton 1962, 141). Consequently, Newton is reluctant to determine positively the nature of bodies, and his analogy would promise nothing but an account of what bodies *could* be (Newton 1962, 138). But we simply have no alternative. The nature of physical bodies is ultimately only discoverable through our inner psycho-physical experience of being coherent units or 'wholes', of being solid and of being capable of exerting force on other bodies through our own purposive, vital activity, i.e. through our human actions. If it were known to us exactly *how* we move our own bodies, Newton says, all other movements would be much clearer (Newton 1962, 141). But still, Newton insists, the analogy between our faculties and the Divine faculties "is greater than has formerly been perceived by Philosophers" (Newton 1962, 141). Furthermore, we do have one tool to help us evaluate whether our analogies could pass as a possible account of 'real' nature: our senses. For "whatever reality we attribute to bodies arises from their phenomena and sensible qualities", Newton says (Newton 1962, 140), and it is the senses "which constitute the sole judges in this matter" (Newton 1962, 139).

Even though Newton's theory of bodily knowledge is brief, it is interesting because it shows the scientist's concern about the trend towards non-realism that lies at the root of the mechanical sciences. Newton seems to have understood that if we accept dualism and reject the experience of our own bodily agency, we will be tempted to deny any activity in the movements of all physical objects in favour of a relativist and structuralist view of nature. But if this be the case, movements will only be movements relative to our thoughts, as they were in Descartes' physics. Newton seems to have concluded that in order to hold on to realism we will have to oppose the early modern tendency to decontextualize or emancipate the cognitive subject from its physical existence. Rather than constructing a view from nowhere, we should accept and cooperate with the natural or 'vulgar' inclinations in our cognition, among which is the tendency ultimately to base all knowledge on the sensational experience of our living and acting body.

7. After *On gravitation*

What became of *On gravitation*'s natural philosophy two or three years on, when Newton published his *Principia*? Concepts like absolute space, absolute time and absolute motion are introduced in a *Scholium* right after the initial definitions of *Principia,* but nothing is mentioned about their ontology. In order not to get involved in controversies, Newton developed what I. Bernard Cohen has called the "Newtonian Style". This was a defensive procedure, which stressed the mathematical dimension of science in order to underexpose or veil the philosophical and even the physical dimensions of the book. The strategy was exercised particularly when Newton touched upon highly controversial subjects like attraction.[18]

Not until the *General Scholium* – an addendum to the second edition of the book – do we learn that God, by enduring and being present everywhere, "constitutes duration and space" (Newton 1999, 941). Newton does not mention emanation, but the theological basis of his natural philosophy is now painted with much more powerful brushstrokes than in the first edition of the work. In *On gravitation* this basis was indeed present, as when Newton expressed his fear that Descartes' deistic mechanics offered a "path to Atheism" (Newton 1962, 143). In the *General Scholium* Newton's antipathy against mechanics is overt, and his countermove against it is a dominant God, the designer and Lord of all. God is living, intelligent, and powerful, and he is 'substantially' omnipresent, "for action requires substance. In him all things are contained and move, but he does not act on them nor they on him" (Newton 1999, 941). Does the 'substantial' presence mean that God is a psychophysical being? Not at all: "he is all eye, all ear, all brain, all arm, all force of sensing, of understanding, and of acting, but in a way not at all human, in a way not at all corporeal, in a way utterly unknown to us ... he totally lacks any body and corporeal shape" (Newton 1999, 942). On the basis of this, Newton disqualifies our knowledge of "the substance of any thing" as we have no "direct sense and there are no indirect reflected actions by which we know innermost substances" (Newton 1999, 942). But Newton still accepts the analogical inference from human beings to God, because even when humans are not as perfect as God, there is "nevertheless a similitude of some kind" and "to treat of God from phenomena is certainly a part of natural philosophy" (Newton 1999, 943). But Newton seems to trust much less in this analogy than he did in *On gravitation*, and – this being so – much less in the analogy likening the human body to bodies in general.

One interpretation of this change is that Newton – triggered by the attacks on attraction he had to put up with after the publication of *Principia* – reinforced his style and public attitude, increasing an impression of positivism or agnosticism. This interpretation is supported by the famous words on the use of *hypothesei* from the *General Scholium*. Another interpretation could be that Newton gave up the destruction of psycho-physical dualism and returned to a dualistic ontology of passive matter and external spiritual activity.[19] The final paragraph of the *General Scholium* and the added *Queries* of Newton's *Opticks*, all from Newton's later years, hint to a third possible interpretation, namely, that Newton entertained a growing concern about the problem of organic life, raised by materialistic traits following in the wake of a mechanical world view. In the very last paragraph of *Principia*, Newton presents a "certain very subtle spirit" that allegedly lies behind phenomena like attraction, chemical cohesion, electricity and light, as well as behind sensation and our movements (Newton 1999, 943-44). This subtle, vegetative spirit or 'æthereal medium' was already introduced in the second edition of the *Opticks* (Newton 2003, 349), and is there connected to a variety of physical phenomena through rhetorical questions ('Queries'). Is this ether responsible for gravitation, refraction, fermentation and cohesion? And is it even the basis for physiological phenomena like sensation, the movements of organisms and the intentional actions of human beings? (Newton 1999, 350ff.). Newton refrained from answering these questions and again expressed his caution about hypotheses not supported by experiments (Newton 1999, 404). But what is this subtle spirit? In Dobbs' interpretation it "inhabits a grey area between the corporeal and the incorporeal" but is nevertheless physical (Dobbs 1982, 249). If this interpretation is correct, Newton may not have given up his struggle with the Cartesian dualism. And maybe this is why, in the same context, Newton again pointed to the analogy between the experience of our intentionally moved body on the one hand and action and change in the world on the other (Newton 2003, 403). The analogy, however, was not developed further.

8. After Newton

Newton's policy of secrecy concerning his natural philosophy made it all too easy for most of his adherents to use his name to authorize a unilateral positivistic interpretation of science ('Newtonianism'). Attention was turned away from causes to (the mere mathematical calculation of) effects.[20] David Hume's critique of causality exposed the weakness of this development, even though Hume himself supported it.[21] His empiricism precluded experience of anything but sequences of effects that could be observed from an external spectator's position. And the suggestion that we might know of causal powers from the ability to command our bodily actions Hume rejected by claiming that, if this was possible, we should have access to the "mysterious" or "secret union of soul and body".[22] For all his differences from Descartes, Hume's general argument and mystification of forces, powers and causes presupposes a Cartesian dualism. Interestingly, one of Hume's contemporary critics, Thomas Reid (1710-1796), rediscovered the embodied knowledge. For Reid it was our bodily intervention in nature that gave epistemological access to causality. We would know of nothing but effects following each other, if the "motions of my body" and "our own constitution didn't convince us that every event have a cause" (Reid 1788, 1, ch. 5).

The balance in favour of structural physics over dynamical physics occasioned eventually a substitution of causality with natural laws. These laws described functional relations between events, and gave no report on any asymmetry between cause and effect. It was not until the twentieth century that references to body and action again surfaced in the analysis of causation. In 1971 G.H. von Wright proposed an interventionalist or 'manipulative' theory of causality in order to answer Hume's skepticism. Von Wright claimed that "the idea of a causal or nomic relationship can be said to depend on the concept of action" (v. Wright 1971, 72).

In phenomenological philosophy, the embodied knowledge has been developed by several authors of which M. Merleau-Ponty is the most familiar. Of more interest to the theme of the present article is Hans Jonas' philosophy that restores the central role of embodied knowledge for philosophy of nature in general, and for understanding the phenomenon of life in specific. In Jonas' 'existential' interpretation of biology, he claims that the elimination of embodied, 'inward' knowledge has confined scientific biology to the "physical, outward facts", and, in doing so, has "submerged the distinction of 'animate' and 'inanimate'". Due to this deficient experience not only has biology forfeited the view of its proper object, the phenomenon of life, but so too has science lost the access to the dynamics of nature as such (Jonas 1966, ix).[23] A final example can be found in the philosophy of Gernot Böhme. In his philosophy of nature the human body plays a pivotal role in the rediscovery of nature as nature, and as an alternative to science's reduction of nature to *techne* (Böhme 1992).

Literature

D'Alembert, Jean (1743 [1968]), *Traité de dynamique* (New York & London: Johnson repr. Corp.).

Bacon, Francis (2000), *The new organon* (Cambridge: Cambridge University Press).

Boudri, J. C. (2002), *What was Mechanical about Mechanics?* Boston Studies in the Phil. of Science (Dordrecht: Kluwer).

Böhme, G. (1992), "Leib: Die Natur, die wir selbst sind" (Body: the nature, we ourselves are), in *Natürlich Natur* (Frankfurt a.M.: Suhrkamp).

Carrier, Martin (1994), "Passive Materie und bewegende Kraft: Newtons Philosophie der Natur", in: Schäfer and Ströker 1994.

Cohen, I. Bernard (1999), "A Guide to Newton's Principia", in: Newton 1999.

Dear, P. (ed.) (1997), *The Scientific Enterprise in Early Modern Europe* (Chicago: University of Chicago Press).

Descartes, René (1644), *Principia Philosophiae* (*PPh*), http://archimedes.mpiwg-berlin.mpg.de/cgi-bin/toc/toc.cgi?step=thumb&dir=desca_princ_081_la_1644 (accessed on 2008-03-21).

Descartes, René (1998 [1647]), "Les Principes de la Philosophie", *Oeuvres philosophiques III* (Paris: Classiques Garnier).

Descartes, René (1997), *Oeuvres philosophiques I* (Paris: Classiques Garnier).

Descartes, René (1998), *Oeuvres philosophiques III* (Paris: Classiques Garnier).

Dobbs, B.J.T. (1982), "Newton's Alchemy and His Theory of Matter", in: Dear 1997.

Dobbs, B.J.T. (1991), *The Janus Faces of Genius. The Role of Alchemy in Newton's Thought* (Cambridge: Cambridge University Press).

Dobbs, B.J.T. and M.C. Jacob (1995) *Newton and the Culture of Newtonianism* (New Jersey: Humanities Press).

Frølund, Sune (2005), *Naturvidenskabens vidensbegreb,* The Danish University of Education, Copenhagen (unpubl.).

Gaukroger, Stephen (2002), *Descartes' System of Natural Philosophy* (Cambridge: Cambridge University Press).

Hall, A.R. and M.B. Hall (1962), in: Newton 1962.

Jonas, H. (1966), *The Phenomenon of Life* (Chicago: University of Chicago Press).

Kant, I. (1997 [1786]), *Metaphysische Anfangsgründe der Naturwissenschaft* (Hamburg: Felix Meiner).

Koch, C.H. (2007), *Natur, videnskab og metafysik. Newton og filosofien* (Aarhus: Aarhus Universitetsforlag).

Koyré, Alexandre (1965), *Newtonian Studies* (London: Chapman & Hall).

Kreimendahl, Lothar (1999), *Philosophen des 17. Jahrhunderts* (Darmstadt: WBG).

Lakoff, G. and M. Johnson (1999), *Philosophy in the Flesh* (New York: Basic Books).

Locke, John (1690 [1979]), *An Essay concerning Human Understanding* (Oxford: Clarendon Press).
Mittelstrass, Jürgen (2004 [1995]), *Enzyklopädie Philosophie und Wissenschaftstheorie I-IV*, Stuttgart, Weimar (Verlag J.B. Metzler).
Newton, I. (1962) *Unpublished scientific papers of Isaac Newton* (Cambridge: Cambridge University Press).
Newton, I. (1999 [1687]), *The Principia. Mathematical Principles of Natural Philosophy, A New Translation* by I. Bernard Cohen and Anne Whitman (Berkeley: University of California Press).
Newton, I. (2003 [1704]), *Opticks*, 1730 edition (New York: Prometheus Books).
Perler, Dominik (1999), "René Descartes", in: Kreimendahl 1999.
Reid, T. (1788), *Essays on the Active Powers of Man,* www.earlymoderntexts.com/reac.html (accessed on 2008-04-16).
Schliesser, E. (2007), "Hume's Newtonianism and anti-Newtonianism", *Stanford Encyclopedia of Philosophy*, http://plato.stanford.edu/entries/hume-newton/ (accessed on 2008-11-15).
Schäfer, L. and E. Ströker (eds.) (1994), *Naturauffassungen in Philosophie, Wissenschaft, Technik III* (Freiburg/München: Verlag Karl Alber).
Schäfer, L. and E. Ströker (ed.) (1996), *Naturauffassungen in Philosophie, Wissenschaft, Technik IV* (Freiburg/München: Verlag Karl Alber).
Spaemann, R. (1987), *Das Natürliche und das Vernünftige* (München: Piper).
Voltaire, F. (1733), *Letters concerning the English Nation,* http://www.fordham.edu/halsall/mod/1778voltaire-lettres.html (accessed on 2008-03-21).
Voltaire, F. (1738), *Élemens de la philosophique de Newton*, http://www.voltaire-integral.com/Html/22/29_Elements_Table.html (accessed on 2008-03-21).
Voltaire, F. (1764), *Dictionnaire philosophique portative*, http://www.voltaire-integral.com/Html/00Table/4diction.htm (accessed on 2008-03-21).
v. Wright, G.H. (1971), *Explanation and Understanding* (London: Routledge).

Notes

1. With the subject's own body as primary experience, Aristotelian epistemology was – so to speak – a natural born ontology and immune to the temptations of anti-realism. Aristotle's concept of nature, however, could not be called 'naturalistic' in the modern sense of that term, based, as it is, on the external observer's view on nature.
2. François de Voltaire (1694-1778) maintained this picture of Newton in his extremely influential books *Letters concerning the English Nation* (Voltaire 1733, no. XIV, XV) and *Élemens de la philosophie de Newton* (written 1735, first published in English 1738 [Voltaire 1738, 148]). Voltaire presented John Locke (1632-1704) as the spokesman of Newtonianism. The picture was confirmed by the French physician and philosopher Jean d'Alembert (1717-1783) in his likewise influential article on 'Attraction' and in his 'Préliminaire' ('*Introduction*') to the *Encyclopédie ou Dictionnaire raisonné des Sciences, des Arts et des Métiers* (1751). See Alexandre Koyré's pivotal analysis of Newton's use of hypothesis (Koyré 1965, 25-52).
3. *Metaphysical Foundations of Natural Science.* Philosophy (metaphysics of nature) works out the foundation for the concepts that are used by science. But science *qua* science does not need this philosophical service (Kant 1997 [1786]), p. XXI).
4. Betty Jo Teeter Dobbs' seminal works *The Foundations of Newton's Alchemy or 'The Hunting of the Greene Lyon'* (1975) and *The Janus Faces of Genius. The Role of Alchemy in*

Newton's thought (1991) seem to have convinced most Newton scholars of the importance of alchemy for Newton's entire *oeuvre*, even if Newton himself consciously veiled this side of his face. I. Bernard Cohen – the author (with Anne Whitman) of the new translation into English of *Principia* (Newton 1999) and of the extensive and authoritative *A Guide to Newton's Principia* – has discarded his original opposition to Dobbs' research , and now accepts the association of the great scientist with alchemy (Cohen 1999, 58ff.).

5. All three editions of *Principia* that Newton was in control of (1687, 1713, 1726), displayed the words 'Philosophiae' and 'Principia' in large capital letters in contrast to the smaller letters of 'Naturalis' and 'Mathematica'. The third edition even displayed as half title: "Newtoni PRINCIPIA Philosophiae/Newton's Principles of Philosophy". Newton probably tried to stage a replacement of Descartes' work with his own but also worked to cover up the vast influence from the philosopher on his own theory (Cohen 1999, 43-48). The creators of Newtonianism preserved this image and spurned the idea of an influence from Descartes. François de Voltaire wrote in his *Dictionnaire philosophique portative/Portable philosophical dictionary* (1764): "He [Newton] never followed him [Descartes], never explained him nor even refuted him. He hardly knew him" (Voltaire 1764, entry: "Cartesianism").

6. Part of *On Gravitation* has recently been translated into Danish in Koch 2007.

7. In *Principias*'s first edition Newton was very careful to stress his ignorance of the true cause of attraction, which is the force behind gravitation and centripetal movements. In restricting himself to presenting only the *mathematical* principles of physics, however, he disclaimed any obligation to explain this cause, which a genuine philosophy of nature would have to (Author's Preface; Book I, sect.11, Scholium [Newton 1999, 381ff., 561]). The famous renunciation of *hypothesei* on the cause of gravitation was added in the second edition of *Principia* (1713). Newton wanted to fend off criticism (from Cartesians and Leibniz) of having reintroduced attraction as an 'occult quality' in natural philosophy. His intention was never to condemn the search for causes in physics, as Locke, Voltaire, d'Alembert and (later) Positivists interpreted him as saying (cf. ref. No. XVII). Newton simply "had not yet assigned a cause to gravity" (p. 943; cf.Dobbs 1991, 188).

8. The ether-theory was presented in the added "Queries" of the Latin edition of *Opticks* (1706) and in its second English edition (1717).

9. I. Bernard Cohen accepts Dobbs' dating of *On gravitation* (Cohen 1999, 58), whereas C.H. Koch takes the "traditional, Aristotelian terminology" of the text as an argument for dating the text back to the 1660s (Koch 2007, 91). Dobbs narrows the dating down to between December 1684 and the early spring of 1685. She suggests the text was intended as a first draft of an introduction to *Principia* (Dobbs 1991, 141).

10. *Principia Philosophiae* (Descartes 1644). References will give the part of the book and the number of the section (such as *PPh*, 2, 28). Important differences between the Latin original and the French translation (supervised by Descartes himself, 1647) will be mentioned.

11. "materie coeli fluida est" (*PPh*, III, 28; cf. III, 24). The presence of an ether allows Descartes to restrict physical interaction to 'impulse' or contact action, i.e. to exclude attractive forces.

12. See the entries "Kinematik", "Dynamik" in Mittelstrass 2004.

13. In a letter to Princess Elisabeth (to whom the *Principia* is dedicated) Descartes writes: "I believe that we have confused the notion of the force by which the soul acts in the body with that by which one body acts on another" (21 May 1643 [Descartes 1998, 21]). A month later he writes: "That is why those who never philosophize but are only aware of their senses do not doubt that the soul moves the body and that the body has impact on the soul. But they consider the one and the other as one thing, i.e. they observe their union. (…) And the metaphysical

thoughts, which engage the pure understanding, serve to make the concept of the soul familiar. And the study of mathematics, which primarily engages the imagination in considering figures and movements, accustoms us to make distinct concepts of bodies. And, finally, by using only life and ordinary conversation, and by desisting from meditations and studies of the things which engage the imagination, one learns to apprehend the union of the soul and the body" (28 June 1643 [Descartes 1998, 44]).
14. *Le Monde*, ch.VII (Descartes 1997, 350). See also Gaukroger 2002, 99.
15. This is the background of Aristotle's teleology.
16. This is why Voltaire and d'Alembert – mistaking Descartes' stance for Newton's – claim that physics is about facts and effects, not about causes (Voltaire 1733, XIV, XV; Voltaire 1738, 148; d'Alembert 1743, XI). Compare also John Locke: "Action, yet truly it signifies nothing, but the effect" (Locke 1690, 294). (Cf. ref. No. VII.)
17. Accordingly "God alone is the true cause of everything which is or can be" (*PPh*, I, 24).
18. Cohen defines "the Newtonian style" like this: "to consider mathematically a concept banned from scientific discourse by the adherents of the mechanical philosophy ... by restricting the level of discourse to mathematical systems which were analogies of physical systems" (Cohen 1999, 149). Newton announces in the *Preface* to *Principia* that he will "concentrate on *mathematics* as it relates to natural philosophy" (Newton 1999, 381). Newton's introduction of 'centripetal forces', alias 'attractions', gives a good example of his defensive style. Firstly, Newton explains that physicians might prefer to call 'attractions' 'impulses' (as if it was just a question of a word). He then continues to downplay physics: "For here we are concerned with mathematics; and therefore, putting aside any debates concerning physics, we are using familiar language so as to be more easily understood by mathematical readers" (Newton 1999, 561).
19. Cf. Carrier 1994.
20. "The concept of force was until the middle of the 18th century considered the *cause* of the effect, whereas force today is *defined by the effect*, which is acceleration: $F = ma^2$" (Boudri 2002, p. 2).
21. Cf. Schliesser 2007.
22. (Hume 1979 [1748], Sect.VII, part 1). Hume, of course, did not know Newton's *On gravitation*.
23. A few quotations give an idea of Jonas' view: "The experience of living force, one's own namely, in the acting of the body, is the experiential basis for the abstractions of the general concepts of action and causation" (p. 22); "Causality is primarily a finding of the practical, not of the theoretical self, of its activity, not of its perception" (p. 23); "the living body is the archetype of the concrete" (p. 23). A contemporary approach to embodiment is Lakoff and Johnson's *Philosophy in the Flesh*. This is, however, based on a traditional 'spectators' concept of external experience (cognitive science) of its object and is hence unable to overcome Cartesian dualism, even if this is the authors' intention. The dualism is rather concealed, as when the authors use words such as 'mental' and 'neural' synonymously (Lakoff and Johnson 1999, 11).